I Have to Call
Someone
Mama

*A grandmother's story of the deception
and deliverance of two siblings rescued from
Munchausen's by Proxy abuse*

TAMMY EADY WALKER

ISBN 978-1-64079-498-6 (Paperback)
ISBN 978-1-64079-499-3 (Digital)

Christian Faith Publishing, Inc.
296 Chestnut Street
Meadville, PA 16335
www.christianfaithpublishing.com

Printed in the United States of America

Table of Contents

Foreword

Twenty-five years ago, I used the word "daunting" when I spoke and wrote about a recently-recognized form of maltreatment called Munchausen syndrome by proxy (abbreviated as MBP). The phrase "medical child abuse" is being used increasingly, at least among legal professionals, to describe this highly disturbing yet underrecognized behavior. Still, that same word—*daunting*—clearly applies today regardless of the precise terminology used. Research into the phenomenon has been constrained for many reasons, especially the consistent refusal of perpetrators to admit to the abuse, let alone allow mental health professionals to explore their possible reasons for abandoning the typically protective maternal role. But Tammy Walker's book, which compellingly describes a true-life case from the perspective of a loving grandmother, will go a long way toward help to demystify MBP and educate the public and professionals fortunate enough to come across it.

Marc D. Feldman, M.D.,
University of Alabama, Tuscaloosa

Preface

I am not a writer. I do, however, have a story to tell. On so many occasions, when I have shared the triumphs of my grandchildren's lives, I have been encouraged to write about it. Our story is from the perspective of a mother and a grandmother. A story of a grandmother who, through tragedy, became their mother in triumph. A story of two children rescued from the abuse of a mother who sought to make them sick so she could satisfy her pathetic need for attention. This abuse is called Munchausen Syndrome by Proxy.

PART 1
The Tragedies

CHAPTER 1

The Paradigm Shift (the Moment I Knew)

You know that moment in a movie when all of the sudden you realize that everything you thought were true is really a lie? Like in the movie, *The Sixth Sense*, when you suddenly realize that Bruce Willis actually was the "dead people" that Haley Joel Osment had been seeing. Bruce didn't even know he was dead. Looking back, it was so obvious. All the signs were there. Bruce was the only one who didn't know he was dead. Come to think of it, in this movie, even Haley Joel exposed a mother with Munchausen's Syndrome by Proxy. What a paradigm shift. When I watched the movie the second time, it was so obvious what was going on. All of the sudden, everything made sense. Things were so clear. That is how things appeared after I realized that my grandchildren were sick because their mother was making them sick. My eyes were opened when I discovered all the lies about their health, all the lies about Trisha's past, her family, her false allegations, her faked accidents, stories of injuries, staged home robberies, her constant ploys to demand attention, and her pouting when someone else received attention even if that someone was her own child at their birthday party. All of her attention-seeking behavior, each and every time was becoming more and more desperate for people to believe her lies and shower her with attention and sympathy.

That is how it was when all of the lies Trisha had told were brought to light. All these flashes of stories she had told me, in my head, I would think, *Oh that was a lie, and that was a lie, and oh that was a lie too.* It all made sense, why she never wanted me to talk to her mom. Why she didn't want me to talk to my son because her story would not match his. The funny thing is, even after I had discovered that almost every thing she had ever told me was a lie, I was still surprised when I suddenly had the realization that something else was a lie. I remember her adoptive mother telling me that nothing surprises her anymore when it comes to Trish. She also told me how to tell when Trish was lying, "Her lips were moving."

Sadly, even after I came to the realization that Trish was the one hurting the children, there was still a small shadow of doubt, of hope, that maybe, it was all a mistake. This was denial, I knew that, but even in the middle of the denial, I wanted to believe something different, something not quite so horrible. The Munchausen Syndrome by Proxy (MBP) offender is so convincingly cunning and crafty at the scheme of manipulation that part of you really does believe their lies even with undeniable evidence that it is indeed just that. I was told this is also why in some MBP cases they will not even consider placing the children with a deceived relative for fear they may continue to believe and enable the abuser. What it took for me to finally stop denying the truth was the fact that the children began to get well when their mother had no contact with them. This coupled with a stack of medical records that I was finally able to review.

Some people have asked me on occasion why I did not report her myself. Mostly because I did not know what was happening. I just could not imagine someone intentionally hurting their child for attention. How could I know? It took three years of hospitalizations for the doctors to finally suspect she was the cause of my grandson

Zander's health issues. Even then, they did not figure it out until she escalated and started making Arianna, her second child, her second victim as well. She was so good at the game but her lies finally caught up with her. She was ultimately caught when a rather unsuspecting intern heard her tell a puzzling lie.

Trish had presented Arianna to the Eglin Air Force Base Emergency Room with claims she had not had a bowel movement in over a week. Arianna was eventually transferred to Sacred Heart Children's Hospital in Pensacola. After several days of hospitalization and even a scope in her bowels to see if she was impacted, the doctors determined that she could go home. For an MBP abuser, this is the worst news possible, that their child is now well and can go home. Just when they are getting exactly the attention they sought, the doctors tell them they can go home. It is like ripping the needle out of the arm of a junkie. It is then that the abuser gets even more desperate to create another problem or insist that the child is indeed not well and the doctors have missed something and must take another look. This is where, in her repugnant, utter lack of hope for more attention, she made her ultimate mistake. It was one intern who thought something did not seem quite right. It was a doctor who went with her gut, even when several Florida Department of Children and Families (DCF) social workers did not believe her, that ultimately became the saving voice for these children. This is our story.

CHAPTER 2

What is Munchausen Syndrome and Munchausen Syndrome by Proxy?

Before I tell you our story, let me start by telling you a bit about Munchausen Syndrome (MS) and Munchausen Syndrome by Proxy (MBP). This is often referred to as a factitious disorder "imposed on self" or factitious disorder "imposed on another." Although I am obviously not a doctor or specialist in the field, when faced with the trauma that my own grandchildren were victims of this abuse, I sought to learn everything I could possibly learn on the subject.

Munchausen Syndrome, commonly referred to as a factitious disorder, is defined as a psychiatric behavioral disorder in which a person feigns illness or disease, fabricates a personal or psychological trauma, or feigns an injury often even inflicting an injury on themselves for the purpose of gaining attention or sympathy. Patients have a history of continually seeking medical attention, seeking out different doctors and hospitals until they find someone who will "treat" them. The pattern of frequenting multiple physicians and hospitals also enables the patient's behavior to remain undiscovered. Being in the patient role, the attention seeker is finding actual comfort and relishes in the attention and sympathy they receive. Patients are often very familiar with medical terminology and request costly and unnecessary testing. If medical staff decline the tests, the patient becomes more and more emphatic, exaggerating symptoms, demanding treatment, and even threatening a lawsuit until the treating physician approves treatments, tests and medication. Munchausen is not like other psychiatric disorders such as malingering in which the patient's goal is to gain something for material gain such as money, drugs, or absence from school or work.

A similar behavior called Munchausen Syndrome by Proxy (MBP) is when a parent or guardian of a child or other person in their care does the same to another person, usually their child, in an attempt to seek attention or sympathy. This is a form of child abuse and in some cases, can lead to death or other serious damage to the child. The majority of MBP offenders are most often the child's mother, who appears to be moving heaven and earth to find the root of their child's illness. The abuser will either inflict an illness or injury on a child, or falsely claim an illness or symptoms so that his or her child will undergo unnecessary and uncomfortable procedures for the purpose of the abusers insatiable need for attention. The abuser is almost always the only witness to the alleged "symptoms," for example: seizures, vomiting, lethargy, apnea, or sudden weight loss (usually brought on by starving the child.) In some cases, a disease or symptom may actually be initiated in the child at the hands of the parent or guardian by intentionally introducing toxins or bacteria to the child.

As suspected in my story, it is believed that my grandchild's mother continually overdosed him on medications that he was already prescribed, for example: liquid albuterol for asthma, or tegratol or clonidine for alleged "seizures." The medication will show up in the blood test, but when found in high doses, an assumption is made that the kidney or liver is not effectively processing the medication, resulting in an overdose. In a majority of cases, the MBP behavior is not identified until a child dies or a sibling suddenly is presented with the same "mysterious" and unexplainable illness. It has been suggested that this disorder should be renamed "medical abuse" to bring to the attention the actual harm caused by the deception, and to make it more difficult for an abuser facing actual child abuse charges to use a "psychiatric illness" as a defense.

Dr. Marc Feldman, M.D., a Clinical Professor of Psychiatry, has written several books on the subject. In his book, *Playing Sick: Untangling the Web of Factitious Disorder, Munchausen Syndrome, Munchausen by Proxy and Malingering*, Chapter 10, page 121–122 he describes MBP :

"In Munchausen by proxy (MBP), individuals create symptoms of illness not in themselves, but in dependent others who serve as "proxies." The majority of MBP perpetrators are women, most often mothers, who induce illness in their children or subject them to painful medical procedures in a quest for emotional satisfaction, such as attention from and control over others. MBP is a form of maltreatment (abuse and neglect), not a mental disorder..."

He further states, "MBP is not a mental illness even though the behaviors and motives are similar to factitious disorder, which is a mental illness. The critical difference is in who is harmed: oneself (factitious disorder) or someone else (MBP). An analogy might help. Barring an accident, if a person shoots herself, we can usually assume she is psychiatrically ill (probably suicidal). But, without instigation if she shoots someone else, we can generally assume that she is not mentally ill. It is much more likely that she is homicidal. Being homicidal does not qualify as an emotional ailment. However being suicidal does. By aiming her deceptions at her child, not herself, the MBP perpetrator unmasks herself as a perpetrator, not a patient. Her actions constitute abuse, not mental disease."

Originally, the term "Munchausen Syndrome" was used for all factitious disorders. Recently, however, there is considered to be a wide range of factitious disorders. The term or diagnosis of "Munchausen Syndrome" is reserved for the most severe form, where the simulation of disease and demand for attention is the driving force of the affected person's life.

There are multiple alarming symptoms or behaviors a patient may exhibit that lead the medical staff to consider the possibility of Munchausen Syndrome or Munchausen Syndrome by Proxy (MBP). Symptoms include but are not limited to: frequent and long history of hospitalizations, patient having a vast medical knowledge of several illnesses including their symptoms and the tests required to confirm these illnesses, frequent requests for medication such as pain killers, requests for a particular treatment plan or a procedure to be performed, an eager openness for extensive invasive surgery, and fabricated stories about personal tragedies, traumas or illnesses. Because MBP abuse is very difficult to prove, the offenders are not often prosecuted without irrefutable evidence such as an autopsy or a video of the abuser actually inflicting harm or administering poison or toxins to the patient.

In the case of my grandchildren, their illnesses and alleged symptoms vanished when they were removed from their mother. Additionally, after an eight-week separation the children were returned to their mother briefly and my grandson was admitted that same evening to a children's hospital with his mother claiming he had alleged "seizures" and lethargy. When the children were removed again six weeks later they once again thrived. The ruling judge in this case stated that although the MBP abuse could not be proven, that this "speaks volumes." He was not willing to keep the children in a situation that could be life threatening. In another recent case a mother, whose name I will not provide, was prosecuted and convicted for killing her son by poisoning him with a salt substance. She had solicited much attention and sympathy on Facebook and other social media. Sadly, this case ended with the loss of the life of a child.

CHAPTER 3

The Houseguest

It was the end of the school year in 2002. Kevin's High School graduation was just a few weeks away. Shortly after that, he would be leaving for boot camp for the U.S. Air Force in San Antonio Texas. I had not wanted him to enlist but he was insistent. He felt it was his duty. It had not even been a full year since the tragedies of September 11, 2001 and he felt this was what he was called to do. This is how he could make a difference. There was no talking him out of it.

He had been dating Trisha since the beginning of his Senior year. She seemed like a nice young girl. We had not spent much time with her. She had graduated midterm and was working for her aunt who had a care home for special needs children. Her parents, who adopted her when she was eight years old, also ran a care home for special needs children. I did not know much about her parents, only that she claimed she did not get along with them and moved in with her aunt shortly after she graduated from High School the previous January.

Kevin had been out with Trisha when he called frantically. He went on to tell me that Trisha's aunt had just kicked her out of the house and she had nowhere to go. She had nowhere to sleep tonight. I reluctantly told him she could stay the night but he would need to sleep downstairs on the couch and give her his room for the night.

They arrived a few minutes later. Trisha was noticeably shaken and very withdrawn. She was rather shy and insecure and she clung to Kevin as he walked with her into the kitchen. I could see that she had been crying but I didn't mention it. We sat in the living room and they told me all about the fight Trisha had with her aunt. He told me that her aunt insisted that she work as many as sixteen hours a day and would not pay Trisha her fair wages. Trisha said she had enough and when she confronted her aunt, she was told she had to leave the house that very hour. I couldn't understand how she could put an eighteen-year-old girl out of her home this late knowing she had nowhere to go. Well, at least I knew she was safe for tonight. I was hoping that perhaps the two could patch things up in the morning.

The next morning came, and Trisha continued to act like a puppy who had been beaten. She toed around like she was terrified of us at first. She was too shy to even sit at the table to eat with us. One day eventually turned into the next; and a week later, Trisha still had nowhere to live. Since Kevin would be leaving for boot camp any day, I decided it would be okay if Trisha stayed with us for a little while. Kevin would not be using his room anyway and I thought I would enjoy not only getting to know this sweet girl, but doing something to help her get on her feet. She appeared to be so tragically broken and sad.

My heart broke for her. I did not know it at the time, but I was about to take a long ride of sick manipulating deception. How could I know that this girl was going to make up story after story, lie after lie, and convince me that she was such a poor mistreated girl that was no longer loved by the family that adopted her at eight years old. How could I possibly know that she would eventually marry my son, have his two children, and then slowly do everything in her power to make them sick, to keep them sick, to continuously poison them, and to bring them literally to death's door step while lying about their medical history to countless doctors, only to feed her pathetic need for sympathy and attention? How could anyone foresee that?

A few weeks later, Kevin left for boot camp. We had gone the evening before to witness him sworn into the US Air Force. I was proud of him, but consumed with worry at the same time. He was my only child and it broke my heart to see him leave home. Why did he have to leave home just three weeks after High School graduation? It didn't take long after Kevin left for Trish and I to bond. She seemed to be such a shy and broken girl. She was even more embarrassed to eat with us now that Kevin had left.

During the months to come, Trisha started to open up and share things with me. She told me stories of horrifying things that had happened to her in her childhood. She had a long surgical scar on her neck and another one in the thoracic area of her upper back. She also had a pronounced gait and drug one foot as she walked. She told me that the surgical scar on her neck was from a cheerleading accident and that she had fallen from the top of the pyramid and hit her head. She said that the scar on her back was from an auto accident where she had been walking home from school and was struck by a drunk driver. My heart sank as she went into riveting detail of the day she was hit. She said her mother just happened to drive by as she was lying in the middle of the road. She explained the horror on her mother's face as she arrived on the scene of the accident. Later, she shared that she really did love her mother, but her mother just did not want her around. I found it unsettling and wanted to help her reach out to her family and find some healing.

Trisha came to our home with just a few articles of clothing. She shared how she really didn't have many clothes, and no one had ever bought her nice things as a girl. The mom in me, the mom that always kind of wanted a daughter to spoil, enjoyed taking her shopping and buying her nice things to wear. It was such a simple thing I could do and it brought her so much joy to receive the gifts. When we got home, she tried on every single outfit and modeled them for me.

"Look, Mama," she said, "look, I feel pretty."

"Did she just call me 'Mama?'" I laughed it off and told her she looked pretty.

Within a matter of weeks, Trish continued to call me "Mama." I actually felt really sorry for her. I tried to get her to open up and tell me about her family. She told me that her dad was her father and that she had a younger brother and a younger sister. She said when her dad married her step-mom that she already had four kids of her own, and that her step-mom insisted her younger sister go into the foster care system because she did not want to deal with her special needs. That her step-mom would only allow Trisha and her brother to live with them. Wait! I thought she had told me before that she was adopted by her parents at eight years old. I questioned her about this and she quickly and with great detail told me that her dad is actually her biological dad, and that it was her mother that adopted her when she was eight years old. Internally, I questioned why her "step-mom" would make her younger sister go into foster care because she had special needs when her parents took care of several special needs children for a living. *File this one in my memory banks to think about later.*

CHAPTER 4

The Game Begins

Over the next few weeks, she continued to call me "Mama." At first, I honestly did not know what I thought about it. When Kevin would call home, he would say it was cute and not to worry about it. Trisha and I wrote Kevin several letters while he was in boot camp. Trisha loved going places with me and she especially loved attending church with us. One Sunday in particular, she started to sob during the worship time. I comforted her and decided not to bring it up when we got home. I would wait for her to talk to me about her feelings. That same week, we were sitting watching television. We had just watched the first season finale of American Idol and were cheering that Kelly Clarkson had won, although Trisha did insist that Justin was pretty cute. We laughed because by now, I knew just how crazy she was about my son. They were already talking about getting married, which I thought was way too soon, but I was really starting to love this girl. She was laughing and giggling and then suddenly, out of nowhere, her entire mood changed to that of a little girl, kind of like that beaten puppy that had first arrived at our home.

"Mama," she whispered. She was sitting on the couch next to me and scooted over and put her head on my shoulder.

"Mama," still talking in this baby voice with her big blue eyes directly looking into mine, "Mama, I have to tell you something, Mama."

She had my undivided attention. Finally, I thought she would open up to me and I could help her with her pain. She spent about fifteen minutes burying her head in her hands with her feet curled up to her chest and just started weeping. I held her head on my chest and comforted her. She started telling me about how a particular person had molested her since she was eight years old. (I will not name the relation of the person because I now know it was a sick pathetic lie). I sat and comforted her for what seemed like hours. She went into great detail telling me how horrible it was and how it destroyed her childhood. She was very graphic and it just broke my heart to hear. It also really made me angry. I later encouraged her to tell Kevin when he called, and he was equally as angry. *Trisha, however, was getting absolutely everything that she needed. All the attention that she wanted... until she wanted more.*

On another occasion, I had gone out of town to visit my mom and sisters, and Trisha wanted to go with me. While at my mother's house, she would not leave my side. When I walked up to the doorstep to my mom's house, she walked behind me holding on to my right upper arm. She would pop her shy little head around my shoulder and shyly say hello to my family members. She was acting like a frightened child meeting strangers for the first time. *This poor girl*, I thought. What had happened to her to make her so afraid of people and so vulnerable? During the trip, she exhibited her usual behavior of clinging to me. She would sit so close to me on the couch that it was smothering. My heart still broke for her. She just needed love. Several family members also noticed that she was a broken individual in need of reassuring love.

She was a gorgeous girl, an absolutely beautiful young woman. She had the most beautiful deep, blue eyes that could just melt your heart. She had dark brunette hair that she wore upon her shoulders. She just needed love. I thought, perhaps, if I loved this young girl, I could help her heal. I made it my mission to pour as much love into her as I could. We went to lunch, out on shopping trips, and really enjoyed each others company. Trisha had started talking about her Mother and called her occasionally. I encouraged her to go visit her mother more. On one occasion, she came to me crying and told me her mom was in the hospital and had kidney failure. I insisted that I take her to visit her mom, and she said that her family would not allow her to visit. That same week, she told me her mother had a seizure while in the hospital. I continued to insist she go visit her mother but she declined.

Trisha wanted to go with me everywhere I went. She did not want to be left alone. She clung to me in a way that seemed a bit off. On one occasion, she went with me to a medical appointment. She decided to stay in the car while I was in the office. Upon returning to the car, she presented me with horrible looking spots of bruising all over her arms. There were spots of bruising all the way up to her shoulders. I took one look and was ready to take her to the doctor when she suddenly decided I should take her to her mother's house to show her. We went to her mother's house and she inspected Trisha's arms. Her mother did not respond with much alarm. She took Trisha in the back room alone and when they returned, she was ready to leave. When we got in the car, Trisha told me that her mother told her it was an allergic reaction. *It was not until years later when her mother and I actually traded stories that she shared she was positive they were self-inflicted hickies. All of the bruises were in places she only could have reached by literally sucking on her own arms to make bruises. This was Trisha's reaction to me leaving her alone in the car while I went to a medical appointment.*

Trisha did not like it when I left her at home, and would pout if I did not take her everywhere I went. One afternoon, I had made previous plans to sit with my elderly, fragile father-in-law so that my mother-in-law could have a day out with a friend. He wanted me to come alone and help him with some range-of-motion exercises on his legs. Trisha did not like that I was leaving her at home. After I arrived at my in-law's home, Trisha called me screaming that she had broke her knee playing basketball with neighbor friends and had to go to the emergency room right then. I was getting used to her dramatics and told her she would be fine, and I would take a look at it when I returned. She screamed, wailed, and cried that she was hurt so very bad and had no one to take her to the hospital. My brother-in-law happened to show up and offered to stay with my father-in-law, so I left to rush Trisha to the emergency room. She pulled out all the stops, screaming all the way to the ER. She did, however, quiet down when we arrived and just sat and waited. When the doctor examined her, he noticed no visible bruising or swelling at all. He took an x-ray that evidenced no injury, so we went home. That evening, I saw what I thought was her hitting her own knee. When she noticed I had seen her, she said she was rubbing it where it was hurting. The next morning, there was a bit of bruising. This was one of the first times I had seen her inflicting injury on herself but convinced myself I was mistaken.

Over a period of months, she told me her grandmother had died, she was abused in unimaginable ways, she was struggling with bulimia, she had suffered several broken bones as a child *(which is why she said she limped)*, the cheerleading accident that resulted in her neck surgery, the car accident that resulted in her back surgery, she was deathly allergic to cottage cheese *(I actually fell for that one too)*, and countless other stories about horrible accidents and events that had happened to her. She also told me that one of the special needs babies her parents cared for, which was on a ventilator, was actually an older sister's baby who lost oxygen at birth because the doctor was drunk. My heart actually hurt that her poor mother's first grandchild was so critically ill after she had spent her life caring for severely ill children. *Looking back, it is kind of embarrassing that she was able to throw out this bait and reel me in like a prize fish.*

September came and Trisha turned nineteen years old. On the morning of her birthday, she announced that she was now ready to go visit her mom. She asked me to drop her off at her mother's house, but not to go in. She said her mom was really mad that she lived with me and she did not want to upset her more. I started asking her if maybe her mother wanted her to come home now, thinking that was a good thing. She insisted it was not. After dropping her off, I waited for her to call me for a ride home. A few hours later, she called and I went to pick her up. I waited in the car outside like she had asked. Trisha came out with her hands full of gift bags. She came out to the car beaming and could not wait for me to take her "home" to show me her presents. She said she was really surprised that her mother had all those birthday presents for her. I was hopeful that it was the beginning of healing between them and I told her so. Trisha quickly told me that her Mom was jealous of me and that is probably the reason for the gifts. *Looking back, years after all of this deception, I now realize that I was Trisha's puppet and my home was Trisha's stage. Her mother, on the other hand, had her number. Trisha showed up on her birthday for no other reason than to get birthday presents. Nothing more, and then she was done with her mother... for now.*

CHAPTER 5

Becoming Family

When Kevin graduated from boot camp a few months later, Trisha rode with us on the long trip from Northern California to San Antonio Texas. It was nice to see Kevin and spend time with him. During the trip, Kevin and Trisha decided that they wanted to get married. The next two months were spent with them making wedding plans. Trisha had much more contact with her mother now and she was busy helping Trisha make wedding plans. I was starting to get to know her mom and really thought she was a wonderful person. She was nothing like Trisha had described. *I have decided not to use her mother's name in this writing because their family has a lifetime of painful Trisha stories, and they do not want to relive any of them. They no longer have any contact with her either.*

On occasion, when Trisha and I were out buying something for their home, we would pop over to show her mother what we had found. She would be busy making beautiful wedding centerpieces and a lovely floral trellis. She was putting her whole heart and soul into Trisha's wedding. I had hoped Trisha might move back home with her parents since she would soon be married and moving to a military air base in Florida. Trisha did not want to move and would end the conversation when I brought it up. After meeting Trisha's family and realizing they were actually very kind people, I worried a lot about how it must look that she continued to live with me.

Kevin came home on leave that December and they were married during Christmas break. He had to leave to finish tech school just after the New Year. When he finished tech school the following February, he came home to pack up his wife and all their belongings. They left for their new home at Eglin Air Force Base, Florida. Trisha acted like it was going to break her heart to leave our home. She was more upset about having to leave me than she was excited about moving to Florida with her new husband. I have to admit I was a bit relieved to finally have some breathing room. After nine months with Trisha, I was ready to be empty nested.

CHAPTER 6

Coming "Home"

Trisha called me every single day, sometimes multiple times a day. I thought she must be incredibly lonely on the Air Force base and having a hard time making new friends. It was a surprise when about six weeks after they moved to Florida, Trisha called and said she was coming "home" for a visit. I was more surprised when I learned that her visit was going to last for five weeks. She was a newlywed and wanted to come back to California to spend five weeks with her mother-in-law? I was not sure how I felt about it, especially when she showed up with her new and rather large pit bull dog in a kennel. I must say I didn't see that one coming.

While Trisha was visiting, her mother called and asked me to join her and Trisha's aunt for lunch. As we enjoyed lunch, they wanted to talk about Trisha and her behavior. Her mother started by telling me how odd it was that a newlywed would leave her husband for such a long time. I think she could tell that I was now getting a bit exasperated having Trisha back in my home. I wanted to love her, she was now married to my son, but she was exhausting. Her mother shared a bit about how she and her husband adopted Trisha at eight years old. She said she had been such a broken little girl from the very beginning and always had a history of pathological lying and making accusations of various kinds of abuse against multiple family members. She described Trisha as "an empty cup" that could not be filled. She had hoped getting married would actually help her to grow up. They started to share that Trisha had mentioned feeling awkward around my husband. "Wait! What?" I thought. My husband had mentioned to me he did not like how Trisha would sit too close to him on the couch. It would make him actually get up and leave the room. He was not as touched when she had started calling him "Daddy" after living with us for two months.

When they brought this up, I just unloaded. I told them everything that Trisha had ever told me. I shared everything she had said about her dad being her dad, and her mom being her step-mom that did not want her, her "accidents," her abuse, her broken bones, everything. Should I have been surprised to find out that none of it was true? None one word of it. She had never been in an auto accident, was never a cheerleader therefore no cheerleading accident, both her parents adopted her from the foster care system when she was eight years old, and spent a lifetime trying to love and heal her.

In return, what they received back was lie after lie until they were as exasperated as I now was. Her surgical scars were to correct damage from a spinal disease called "syringomyelia" and an issue with her brain stem, an issue she had since birth. Her mother assured me that she personally had never had kidney failure and did not have seizures. This made me angry because my husband actually has seizures and they are frightening to watch him go through. Trisha invented the "seizure" story after I had mentioned my husband had seizures. I had told her about his seizures to prepare her for what to do if she ever witnessed him having one. Her mom shared with me that is called "borrowing." She said that Trisha loves to borrow other people's tragedies. She will hear of someone else's tragedy and instantly turn it into her own. Then I realized that the night she told me she was molested, we had recently seen something on TV with that as a storyline. I asked them if she made up stories about being molested and they confirmed that, yes, she has done that and even been caught and admitted to lying about them. When I shared the story, they were ready to go confront her that evening.

We ended the lunch. We talked later and decided that the lies and allegations needed to be confronted so that she knew that she had been caught. Later that night, her parents came over to confront Trisha. Trisha turned into a raging monster right before my eyes. She was no longer that shy, clingy, little girl I had come to know. I had never seen this side of her before, and it was not just frightening, but eye opening. She said some of the most horrifying things to her parents that evening. The lovely parents that had just paid for an absolutely beautiful wedding for her and had devoted their lives to her. They were devastated! As they left that evening, her mother, in tears, said to me, "Tammy, watch out. She will turn on you. She will try to destroy you." Her mother, her beautiful loving mother, had just had the heartbreak of her life and still possessed the grace to think to warn me. *To this day, no one in her adopted family has ever had contact with her again. They were done! I, on the other hand, had another six years of torment to come.*

After this confrontation, I could not wait for Trisha to return to Florida. I very willingly offered to pay the difference in air fare for her to change her ticket and return home sooner than planned. My poor son, Kevin, what a nightmare we had watched him walk into marrying this girl. I eventually shared everything with him. He believed that Trisha was a liar with a lot of problems but he did not know what he could do.

CHAPTER 7

The First Visit

It was June of 2003 and I went for the first time to Florida to visit Kevin and Trisha. I had never been to Florida and was looking forward to seeing the land. One afternoon, Kevin and Trisha wanted to go scuba diving and we packed a picnic and were on our way to DeFuniak Springs Lake. Just as we were driving around a bend on the Highway, we witnessed an auto accident. One car had slammed off to the right shoulder. We all got out of the car to help. I instantly looked at the car on the right shoulder and saw a woman getting out of the car. "Are you okay?" I asked her. She said she was fine so I scanned to see where the other car had gone. It was all the way in the middle of a rather large grassy division in the road lying upside down.

As I ran to the car, I saw a suitcase, clothing, and other belongings strewn all the way across the road and into the divider. I remember seeing a ziplock bag filled with several biscuits among the items. I approached the SUV and first checked for children in the back seat. When I saw none, I could see that the driver was a female about middle age, laying face down strewn across the vehicle on the ceiling, as the car was upside down. She was shaking and all her limbs were trembling. She was wearing shorts and her shoes had been kicked off and were laying on the ground.

Since I could not get to where her face was without crawling on her, I gently rubbed the back of her calves to reassure her someone was there with her. I thought if she felt some physical touch, it may comfort her since there was not much else I could do. I did find her wallet near by; and out of instinct, opened it and learned that her name was Phyllis. I called her by her name as I said comforting things to her. I saw a check book in her wallet and immediately called the number and left my name and number and the information about the accident. All I could think of is that this woman may be dying and is all alone and someone out there would want to know. It hit me hard, hearing a female voice on the answering machine because I knew it must be her voice. When I hung up the phone, I just continued to pray for her out loud while using her name and rubbing her leg. I watched as the woman's arms and legs slowly stopped moving. I still held out hope that she was alive. I looked up and saw Trisha just staring on with no expression at all and offering no assistance.

Everyone at the scene was doing something to help, except Trisha. The ambulance arrived and Trisha walked over to me while I was still kneeling down over this woman's body and said, "Mom, can we go now? I want to go scuba diving." When we got to the lake, Trisha could not wait to jump in the water and go. I was still in shock over just watching a person die forty-five minutes earlier. I spent the entire day hoping she had somehow survived, but was pretty certain she had not. When I pulled out my sandwich for lunch, I thought of the ziplock bag of biscuits that were on the ground near the accident. *It happens that fast*, I thought, *one minute you are packing your biscuits for a trip and the next minute you are dying.* That evening, it hit me hard and I stayed awake most of the night. I dreamed about the event as I slept. The next day, two different members of her family called to thank me for contacting them. They told me that she did not survive. They asked for details about the last moments of her life. They were comforted by the fact that I had touched her, and used her name while I prayed and talked to her and stayed with her until help arrived. I cried on the phone with her sister-in-law. She kept referring to me as "our angel." I carried this event in my heart for months to come. The reason I share this is because although I know I probably got a bit too emotionally involved and suffered for some time with PTSD, Trisha showed not one feeling or any kind of emotion for what she had seen. Her only concern in the world was getting to that lake.

While still in Florida, Trisha displayed her usual attention-seeking behavior. At one point, she decided her old "knee injury" had flared up and put on a big knee brace and started using crutches. She said there was no way she could put weight on it. When I mentioned that was too bad because Kevin and I were going to go to the water park the next day, her knee got completely better over night. She rode on the water slides all day without one mention of her hurt knee. After a while, I learned not to respond to her attention-seeking behavior.

CHAPTER 8

Becoming a Grandma

A few months had passed and in late 2003, Kevin and Trisha found out they were having a baby. Trisha's pregnancy was surprisingly uneventful other than a few times they were sent to a military base in Boluxi, Mississippi for genetic testing. The tests did confirm that the baby would not have the spinal disease, "syringomyelia," that Trisha actually did suffer from.

In July of 2004, I flew to Florida for the birth of my first grandson, Alexzander. I must say that I did not like the way she chose to spell his name at first, but it did seem to grow on me. They eventually nicknamed him "Zander" rather than the usual nickname of "Alex." "Zander" seemed to fit him. I brought along a quilt I had made him. It was the first quilt I had ever made. Becoming a first time grandmother and having an empty nest brought on a new passion for quilting.

I was happy that Trisha wanted me in the labor and delivery room. We had bonded more over her pregnancy and I had hoped she was growing up a bit herself. Zander's birth had a few scares. During Trisha's labor, his heart rate kept dropping alarmingly low. When it hit eighty beats per minute, the nurses would come in and check on the both of them. The nurse kept telling me, "If I am not worried, you do not need to be worried." I attempted to comfort Trisha through her labor, but I still could not take my eyes off of that heart monitor. After several hours of labor, Zander's heart rate dropped to forty beats per minute. The doctors and nurses all came flying into the room at once, and quickly moved her into an operating room for an emergency caesarean procedure. For every beat his heart rate dropped, I am sure mine was going up just as much. It was only about ten minutes before we heard our Alexzander's first cry.

They brought him into the room and did all the usual exams. When the nurse asked me if I wanted to hold him, I decided that Trisha should be the first one to hold him. She was still not back in the room. When Trisha returned, she told me it was okay for me to be the first one to hold him. I was surprised, blessed, and totally in love with him the moment I saw him. The first thing I noticed is that he had my dimples, which was the first thing my mother said she noticed about me when I was born. He had beautiful blue eyes and blonde hair. The doctors said he was in perfect health with only one small issue. His left leg and foot turned in slightly. The doctor said this may straighten out in time; and if it did not, that he may require surgery when he is older to correct it. After the scare, we had just had with his heartbeat dropping, the news about his leg was rather easy to receive. They gave him a health score called an apgar score. They scored him a 9.9 out of 10. They removed the .1 only because of the issue with his leg, which was not even noticeable to us. Other than that, he was a perfect healthy baby boy.

It was cute seeing Kevin as a new daddy. When they first left the hospital to bring Zander home, he was driving extremely slow. When asked why, he said, " I do not want him to get shaken baby syndrome." We laughed. Obviously, Kevin did not know what that was, but it was adorable seeing him so protective of his new baby. He was a young father, both he and Trisha were just twenty years old when Zander was born. I had become a mother at a young age as well, so I was blessed to become a grandmother at only forty-two years old.

Trisha actually seemed to be attentive with Zander. She appeared to be doing very well caring for him. I stayed and helped her for about two weeks and we really had a great time. When I left Florida, the air base was in the middle of a hurricane warning. It was expected to be a category four hurricane. I hated to leave, but was assured they had safe places to find shelter. I knew that if I did not leave as planned the flights would be cancelled for several days, so I went home, it was time. We later found it funny that the first hurricane right after Alexzander's birth was named Hurricane Alex.

When Zander was just one month old, he was hospitalized. After several tests, including a painful lumbar puncture, Trisha called to tell me the news that he had been diagnosed with meningitis. He was hospitalized for well over a week. I had several friends and church members praying for his recovery. Trisha called me several times a day with updates. Zander was hospitalized one more time a few weeks later with what Trisha had described as "lethargy." She said he would not wake up or eat. I was so worried about him being so very sick as such a young age. Obviously, the doctors wanted to keep a close eye on him since he had just had an awful illness and was just not recovering. Trisha gave me updates on his condition several times a day. I felt completely helpless being so far away and not able to be near him while he was so sick.

CHAPTER 9

Coming Home Plus One

Zander was about three months old when his Daddy was deployed to Iraq. Trisha wanted to come stay with us in California while Kevin was deployed so I flew out to drive back with her. I was thrilled to have the new grand baby with us. I was especially relieved since he had been so sick. Within the first month, Zander was having little fevers here and there but one doctor commented that he was really underweight for his age. Trisha shared that he threw up a lot. I had not seen him do that, but was not with him all the time like she was. Eventually, Zander was referred to a specialist to help him put on some weight. They put him on a formula that added extra calories to each bottle. I tried to help out with the bottles and make them up in advance but Trisha insisted that she make them one at a time. Every time I tried to give him a bottle, she would yell, "Mom, he is going to throw up! I have him on a feeding schedule."

After talking to my husband about this, his response was, "Give me that baby. I am going to feed him."

Trisha did not dare speak to or correct my husband the way she did me. I remember taking a video that day of my husband feeding Zander while he lie on the floor. *Watching that video back years later, we now notice Trisha sulking in the background because her plan to starve that baby was unraveling. My husband fed Zander bottles every day and there was never a word said about it again. That gig was up.*

It was just before Thanksgiving in 2004. The baby was about four months old and was hospitalized for weakness and lethargy. After he had been in the hospital a few days, I offered to stay with him and give Trisha a break, and she flat out refused. "I am his Mama and I need to be here with my baby."

While in the hospital, his doctor came in to see him. He said that Zander showed all the signs of meningitis; and since he had it just a few months earlier, it would be a good thing to check for. The doctor wanted to perform a lumber puncture. I know these are very painful and could not stand the thought of him having to go through that kind of pain. He was just a helpless little baby. I hated to see him lay there with all the needles in his arm. Trish was all too eager to get the test done. She would continually tell me, "Mom, there is something seriously wrong with your grandchild." She said this often like she was trying to convince me and persuade the doctors as well.

When the doctor came in to perform the procedure, he offered Trish the option to leave the room if it was too difficult for her to watch. She not only declined, she wanted to stay and help. I sat in the chair just praying for him. I was a mess. The doctor let Trisha help hold him down while he performed the procedure. She jumped right in and had no problem using her body weight to lean in and hold him down.

"Hold him like a football under your arm," the doctor said.

She held down his head and arms while the doctor inserted the needle. She had a very cold yet satisfied expression while she watched Zander go through this. I listened as Zander would cry out and whimper in pain. I couldn't stand it. I burst into tears. I just sat there quietly as floods of warm tears ran down my cheeks. When it was over the doctor looked at me and said "I don't see many grandmothers react like this. Usually, it is the moms that do." *Little did I know at the time that I was called to be this child's mother, his protector. My soul was already deeply knit to his.*

CHAPTER 10

Calls Home

It was just after the New Year in 2005. Kevin had been in Iraq for about six months. I worried endlessly about him. Each and every day, the first thing I did when I woke in the morning was roll out of bed onto my knees and thank God that he was safe and that I had not received that feared knock at my front door. The knock that I have only seen in movies when the military personnel in full dress uniform arrive with a Chaplin. The family member knows what this means the moment they see them walk up the walk way. Every single evening was the same. I would get on my knees and ask the Lord to continue to protect him and to help ease my worry and trust that Kevin would come home safe. Still, throughout the day, I found myself jolting with fear if the doorbell happened to ring. On occasion, I would ask Trisha how she was handling the stress of Kevin's deployment. I found it shocking when I asked her if she worried about him and she said, "No, he's fine, Mom. Stop being so dramatic! Now, can we go somewhere? I am bored. Can we go to the mall?"

She did not seem to be phased a bit that he was in danger. Not until someone would call to ask her how he was, then she would turn on the water works and tell them how worried she was. It made me sick to see her use his deployment as a means for gaining sympathy from others. Mostly, I was saddened because I knew she really did not care.

To help ease my worry, I would put together care packages for Kevin. For one package, I took a picture of Zander sitting in the empty box with a red bow on his head and then filled the box and put the picture of Zander at the top. I included a note from Zander that said he wanted to come too, but we made him get out of the box. Kevin treasured this picture. I sent him a package every couple of weeks stuffed with snacks, socks, and all the goodies he would ask for during his phone calls home. I longed for his phone calls just to hear his voice. I tried to make every phone call with him as positive as I could to keep him from worrying about his family. I would reassure him that I was taking care of his wife and his infant son. I always tried to offer him emotional support and to let him know I was praying for him. I would only talk to him for a moment when he called before I felt I should give the remaining phone time to Trish. She was his wife after all.

Zander's Care Package

One particular time, when he called, she went in her room to take the call. I went into my room as well. When I walked into my room, I realized that the baby monitor was in my room and I could hear Trisha's side of the conversation. I tried to walk out and not listen, but when I heard her yelling at him and cussing at him, it stopped me cold. She was screaming at him for not calling her more. She was cussing at him and complaining that he spent too much money. Instead of building him up and reassuring him, she was tearing him down, the exact opposite of what I was trying to do. This was eye opening to me because it made me realize that Trisha did not care about Kevin's needs at all. She did not care that she was upsetting him while he was in the middle of a war zone. It did not even cross her mind that each phone call from Kevin could possibly be the last. All she cared about is what affected her and what she wanted. I felt guilty for listening, but I am still glad that I did. It armed me for warfare at home, for spiritual warfare.

On one of Kevin's phone calls, home I got to talk to him for a while. He said that the enemy kept shooting a type of explosive at the chow hall on the base where he was staying. He said they were little ones that didn't really go off and it was mostly annoying and no big deal. "You know, Mom, kind of like a California earthquake." I did not think that was funny or that it was no big deal. I was a worried Mom pacing the floor. I shared this with Trisha and my husband. We prayed for him that evening. It was just a week or so later that I saw on the news that twenty-eight troops were killed when a bomb hit a chow hall on a base in Iraq.

I did not know what base was hit. My husband and I prayed all day. I sat in my living room most of the day facing the window out the front door. I thought, for every minute I do not see a car drive up and uniforms get out, that I knew Kevin was okay. I sat with my phone in my hands the entire day waiting to hear from Kevin. Trisha, however, went to the mall. Later that evening, I learned on the news that it was not the same base where Kevin was stationed. I was quite relieved, but also felt guilty for my relief, knowing that several people *had* lost their loved ones that day. Someone *was* getting that knock on their door. When Trisha came home, I told her the good news. Her response was, "Look, Mom, at the new clothes I got." She had not thought about it or even cared to hear the news that he was okay.

One day, Trisha decided to take a bike ride to the park. She had one of those baby strollers that attached to the back of the bike. She strapped Zander up in the stroller. She also put her dog Gizmo on a leash and rode down to the park with them. About twenty minutes later, I heard her running up to the house frantically screaming, "Mom, they took my baby! They took my baby!"

She was screaming hysterically, several neighbors had come outside of their houses. Tears were streaming down her cheeks. I looked out and saw that she had left the stroller and bike parked in the street right out by the curb.

"Mom, they took my baby," she kept screaming.

By now, multiple neighbors were in our yard wanting to help. I screamed to my husband to come. He already had his keys while one neighbor was calling 911.

I said, "Trisha, who? Did they take Zander?"

"No, Mom, they took Gizmo. They took my baby!"

She was in this frantic state because she said someone had drove up to the park, grabbed her dog, and threw it into the back seat.

"Where is Zander?" I insisted.

"He is in his stroller. Mom they took my baby."

She had left Zander in the stroller on the street, while she ran up to tell me that someone had taken her dog. Within a matter of minutes, the dog showed up and a neighbor knocked on the door to let us know. The neighbors were all still outside talking about how they had all thought the same thing, that Zander had been kidnaped. *Again, looking back, I did not know it at the time, but she had taken my own heart hostage using my love for Zander as a weapon. I do not think any of this story of hers was true. It was all just more theatrics on her stage.*

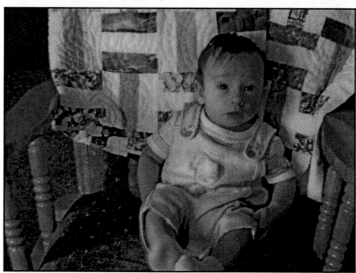

Zander's First Year

CHAPTER 11

"There's Something Seriously Wrong with Your Grandchild"

It was late 2005, and now that Kevin was home from Iraq, they were once again stationed in Florida. Trish called me every single day. Sometimes, multiple times a day. She was still very dependent on me in an unhealthy way. She would tell me every little thing that Zander had done. He had repeated ear infections and continued to be under-weight. I remembered back when he was hospitalized in California, he was not even on the fifth percentile for his weight. Sometimes, Trisha would call me four and five time a day. Most of the times, it was to tell me something was "wrong" with Zander. It seemed like she was always taking him to the doctor or the emergency room for something. I would give her the advice, but usually, she just wanted me to act concerned and worried. After a while, I caught onto her need to exaggerate and would try not to react to her. When I did this, the complaints about his health seemed to always get worse. She would add more and more details until she raised concern in me. I seemed to fall for it every time. I loved that baby so much. I was helpless. If I talked to her about it at least I knew for that moment that he was okay.

In Zander's first two years of life, I could estimate that he was hospitalized more than fifteen times lasting from a few days to several weeks. Each and every time for something that only Trisha had seen the symptoms. Trisha also took him to the emergency room quite often. Trisha would present him to the doctor with alleged lethargy, excessive vomiting, failure to eat, seizures (which only she was witness to), migraines (not sure how she decided that for a two year old), and "accidental" poisoning such as ingesting several iron tablets or allergy medications that had been left out for him to reach. By this time, I had learned to talk to Kevin before I believed anything that Trisha said. Zander was only two years old, yet Trisha had a doctor convinced that he needed to be on seizure medication as well as medication for Attention Deficit Disorder. When Trisha would describe some of Zander's issues, she would use the same phrase over and over again, "Mom, there is something seriously wrong with your grandchild." She never said there was something wrong with "my baby" or something wrong with "Zander." She always said there was something seriously wrong with "your grandchild." She wanted me worried and showering her with attention. That was her goal.

CHAPTER 12

A New "Mama"

Kevin and Trish had just met a new couple on base who lived across the street from them. The couple was older than they were, and had teenagers at home as well as a grown child and granddaughter. Trisha seemed to take to the new woman whom she called Tina. She told me Tina was a nurse and helped her a few times when Zander was sick. It seemed Trisha was now with Tina every time she talked to me on the phone. I noticed Trisha's conversations became very rude, abrupt, and even hostile when she would call me. The only exception to this was when she wanted me to send her money and then it was the baby voice calling saying, "Mama, I don't have diapers" or "Mama, I don't have groceries." I always caved and gave her money at least twice a month. I could not let my grandson go without the things he needed.

It was not long before Trisha was referring to this neighbor woman as "Mama Tina" and then eventually that title had been shortened to "Mama." Where had I seen this before? Trisha had a new "Mama." I was not sure if I was relieved or insulted but I knew that "Mama" was hearing an earful about me. On a few occasions, when Zander was hospitalized, Tina would be the one to call and tell me the news. At one point, Trisha told me that the doctors had determined that Zander had a brain tumor. I had her put Tina the "nurse" on the phone who confirmed to me that she was personally in the room when the doctor told them that Zander had a brain tumor. My entire world fell apart. I had friends and family members praying nonstop. I researched everything I could find about brain tumors. When I asked Trisha what kind of tumor it was, she could give me no further information. Eventually her story changed and she said the doctors had now decided it was a cyst and not a tumor. She said the doctors told her it was an "arachnoid cyst." I researched everything I could find about arachnoid cysts and although this was much better than a brain tumor I did not like this diagnosis either.

In April of 2006, Trisha gave birth to a second child, my granddaughter, Arianna. I had planned to be present for the birth but due to complications, Trisha had an emergency caesarean five days prior to my flight. I had talked to Trisha the night before the procedure that was scheduled for the following morning. The next morning, I got a call from Tina telling me that "we" had a new grand baby. She emailed me several photos as well.

I arrived in Florida a few days after Arianna's birth. She was perfect and beautiful and had my heart the moment I laid eyes on her. She too had my dimples as well as deep blue eyes. We had a lot of fun dressing her up in frilly little dresses and taking photos of her. We probably took a hundred photos that first week. Zander, who was twenty-one months old, was adorable with his little sister. He would walk to her baby swing and gently kiss her forehead and then look over for approval. We let him hold her once to take a photo and noticed that he was doing what appeared to be hitting her, but it was ever so gently. It took us a bit to figure out that he had seen us burp her and he was trying to burp her as well. It was adorable, but we told him he probably should not do that.

After about a week, Trisha started noticing Arianna's color was "off." She would bring her to me and she looked a bit purple, but her color always returned after I picked her up and stimulated her a bit. Arianna was hospitalized shortly after this due to having very low oxygen level in the 80s. Over a period of months, Arianna would have what Trisha referred to as "episodes" of apnea (ceased breathing.) At just a few months old, Arianna was placed on an apnea monitor. Trisha called me multiple times a day to tell me how often the monitor alarm went off. Again, this was another thing that was mostly only noticed by Trisha. I still worried and wanted updates.

When Arianna was five months old, they came to California to visit. While I was holding her, Trisha pointed out that she was having an "episode." No one noticed anything, but Trisha insisted that "There is something seriously wrong with your grandchild." She had said this to me several times before about Zander, but now, she was saying it about Arianna as well. I probably heard her say this a hundred times regarding both children.

"Mom," she said, "Maybe Arianna has the same sickness that Zander has?"

Now that there were two children, they both took turns being hospitalized for various reasons. The bulk of the "illnesses" were still suffered by Zander. When Arianna's first birthday came around, I remember her telling me about the big party they were going to throw. They had ordered cake and decorated and "Mama Tina" was going to have a barbeque at her new house off base. As the time approached, Zander started showing more symptoms of "lethargy." I remember he was hospitalized with Trisha by his side while everyone else celebrated Arianna's first birthday. I was still not fully on to her deception yet, but now believe that there was just too much attention being given to Arianna for her first birthday, and Trisha "needed" Zander in the hospital again.

CHAPTER 13

The Longest Flight

It was early 2007, Zander was just over two and a half years old. A doctor on the Air Force Base had put him on the prescription medication clonidine for what Trisha had described as seizures. For several days, Trisha had called me telling me that Zander was lethargic, slept all day, and at times, was unable to wake up. I told her to take him to the emergency room. When she called me later, she told me the doctor instructed her to discontinue the clonidine as that was the cause of his lethargy, tiredness and extreme weakness. It made sense to me. I had just been reading online some of the side effects and symptoms of overdose of this drug: *Dizziness (extreme) or faintness, unusual tiredness or weakness (extreme), drop in blood pressure, drop in heart rate.* I could not understand why any doctor would put a two-year-old on this medication, but was glad he was no longer going to take it. Within a day, Zander was back to his normal self and doing better.

It had been less than a week when Trisha called me again.

"Mom, Mom, don't freak out," the voice said as I picked up the phone, "Zander is unresponsive. He has no vitals."

"What do you mean he has no vitals?"

"They just said he is unresponsive. They just put him on a helicopter."

Knowing her tendency to exaggerate, I said, "Trish, is he breathing? Tell me if he is breathing?"

"Nope, he just pretty much flat lined."

"What helicopter? Where is he going? IS HE BREATHING?"

Still, no answer to my questions.

"Mom, I have to go now. I have to go home and pack my bag. Then I have to go get gas. It is a sixty-five-mile trip to Pensacola."

"Pensacola? Is that where they are taking him?"

"Yea, Mom, and then I need to go to McDonald's because I haven't eaten anything all day. Can you send me some money for hospital food?"

This was her concern. She needed to pack a bag, get gas, and go to McDonald's. Never mind that her two-year-old was in a helicopter right now and "unresponsive" with "no vitals." She wanted McDonald's!

Knowing that I was getting no answers from her, I hung up. I began calling information to find out what hospital in Pensacola he may have gone to. After several phone calls, I was finally connected with Sacred Heart Children's Hospital in Pensacola, Florida. I told the nurse my grandson was on a helicopter on his way and I needed to know if he was breathing. The nurse told me he should be there soon.

"I need to KNOW if he is breathing? I was told he is unresponsive."

The nurse offered to radio the helicopter and put me on hold. After what seemed like an eternity, she returned, "They said he is awake and crying."

I was so relieved. I immediately called Trish. When she answered I said, "Trish I called the hospital and…"

Trish cut me off and said, "Mom I am in the drive-through I will call you in a little while."

She did not even want to know what I had to say. While she was hitting the McDonald's drive-through, I was the one trying to look up the children's hospital in Pensacola. I was calling the ER and begging them to find out if he was breathing. This is what a mother should have been doing! I *was* his mother! I just did not know it yet.

During this hospitalization, I began to have doubts about the validity and origin of Zander's "illnesses." I talked to Kevin and told him that I was confused about some things. Kevin and I were finally having a private talk for the first time in months. Most of the time, when I talked to him, Trisha was usually screaming at him in the background. I mentioned to Kevin that Zander had gotten better when they took him off the clonidine and wondered if Trisha had given it to him again. Kevin was puzzled.

He said, "Mom, the clonidine is in the diaper bag."

I told Kevin to please ask the doctors to look into it. Kevin's response was that he would talk to Tina about it. He seemed as concerned as I was. It wasn't ten minutes before I got a screaming phone call from Trisha. She called me every swear word you can imagine.

Her first statement was, "Tammy, you are never going to see your grandchildren again."

That is how the conversation began. Interesting that she was suddenly calling me "Tammy" instead of "Mom." I could hear her "Mama" Tina in the background cheering her on.

She went on screaming at me saying how dare I make such an accusation. I told her I was confused why Zander had gotten better off the medication and then suddenly got worse. I asked her why the clonidine was in the backpack. She said the doctor told her to bring it to the hospital and that he "flushed it down the toilet." *You may want to scream at me at this point, but I actually believed her.*

I, once again, fell for her long detailed explanation of what happened and just how sick this baby was. Her explanations always had so many details. She was so convincing! She should have gone to Hollywood and taken up acting. She was that good! I, on the other hand, think I could not truly grasp the unimaginable, that she was hurting him. This, coupled with the threat of never seeing my grandchildren again, was the fear that motivated me to believe her. *In hindsight, I am sickened that I did not go with my original gut on this. After this event, Zander was never the same. When he turned three years old, he still was not speaking a single word. Kevin and I talked about this recently. He mentioned to me that Zander's clonidine was a patch and not a pill so there is no way a doctor had flushed it down the toilet. He also mentioned that Zander had several square rash spots on his back during the hospitalization. Now, we believe that she had put several patches on him at once until he became "unresponsive."*

Kevin was eventually deployed again, but this time, Trisha decided to stay in Florida. She did, however, decide to come to California to visit while he was out of the country. She decided to drive out this time. While she was here, she talked a lot about Zander's health issues and his "seizures." Kevin had told me that he had never seen Zander have a seizure. I asked her what kind of seizures he had, and she responded with "really big ones." She informed me that Zander was now taking tegretal for his seizures since they had taken him off the clonidine. Later this same afternoon, she and Zander had just come back from being out shopping. She brought him back and sat him down for lunch.

She told me, "Look, Mom, look at him. See, he is having a seizure."

His arms were shaking more like a tremor, kind of like a nervous jerk. It was like he was trying to shake off a jerk. I had never seen this jerk before, but it did not look at all like the seizure activity that I had seen my husband have. This was the only time I saw Zander do anything like this. It happened the same day, just a few hours after I had mentioned that Kevin had never seen the seizures, only she had. *This event will come back to me later, when I suddenly realize how she made this happen to him.*

CHAPTER 14

All the Nurses Know My Name

I could not even guess the number of times Zander was admitted to the hospital. Trisha relished in these hospitalizations almost like it was taking a grand vacation. Trisha commented that the nurses were very nice and all of them knew her by name. She was very comfortable in this setting; and although many people offered to come sit with Zander to give her a break, she always abruptly declined. It was very hard being all the way on the other side of the country when he was so often sick. I always felt helpless and worried endlessly. Trisha loved this.

In the fall of 2007, she called to tell me that Zander was once again displaying "lethargy." Over a period of several days, she relayed that his legs were collapsing under him, then his arms, he was vomiting, and unable to walk steady and was displaying difficulty breathing. This unfolded over several days. When she went to Zander's occupational therapy appointment one afternoon, she told me the therapist "went nuts" when she saw his condition. This resulted in once again another hospitalization. Being apprehensive as well as worried sick, I asked her one day if I could confirm his condition with the doctor. She became furious. When I told her that I was thinking about calling the Red Cross and seeing if Kevin could return home, she decided to let me talk to a nurse. A nurse did confirm that Zander had some partial paralysis and described the same symptoms that Trish had described. I contacted the Red Cross who had to confirm the seriousness of the situation to even consider bringing Kevin home. When it was confirmed that Zander's health was grave enough to warrant Kevin coming home, I was once again worried out of my mind.

Over the next week, Trisha told me that the doctors thought Zander had Gillian-Barre Syndrome. This is a very rare disorder where your body's own immune system attacks your nerves. Side effects are weakness in the extremities, which spreads quickly from the lower limbs up to the upper limbs eventually paralyzing your whole body. It can be a life threatening illness and requires hospitalization. I had no reason to doubt Trisha's word because I knew the Red Cross had confirmed Zander's condition prior to bringing Kevin home. *It was not until one year later when I actually read Zander's medical records that I learned what his diagnosis during this hospitalization was. The records said "Guillian-Barre was on the differential, but it was ruled out. Cause of symptoms was a tegretol overdose."* Some of the symptoms of tegretol overdose are dizziness, drowsiness, problems with walking and coordination, nausea, vomiting, shortness of breath, and fainting or feeling lightheaded. Once again, the "overdose" was considered "accidental" because it was a medication that was prescribed to him. I wish I had known this sooner. I wish I had known a lot of things sooner. I believed for a year that Zander had actually had Gillian-Barre Syndrome, Trisha never told me otherwise.

Zander was now three years old and had been hospitalized more times than I could count. He also was not talking at all. Three years old and he had never said one sentence. His language was just sounds. He uttered sounds as his best attempt to communicate. He was very hyperactive, and had severe behavioral issues. Late one night, a woman on base found him walking in the road in the middle of the night. This resulted in a referral to social services. Although Kevin installed more locks on the door that were out of his reach, Zander still managed to move chairs and open doors. Their back door was next to the dryer. Zander would move a chair to crawl up on the dryer. Then stand on the dryer and open the door. He was very difficult to keep up with. He was eventually put back on ADHD medication to help with his behavior. He eloped from the home on more than one occasion.

CHAPTER 15

One Final Bow

Trisha was unaware that the curtain on her stage was about to close. Zander was now receiving physical therapy, occupational therapy, and speech therapy. He still was not talking. I believe since Zander was having so many appointments that Trisha was finding some satisfaction and he was not becoming as "ill" as he had previously been. Although Arianna had been hospitalized a few times before, she was relatively in good health. It was January of 2008 and Arianna was just twenty-one months old. Trisha presented Arianna to the Eglin Air Force Base Emergency Room stating that she had not had a bowel movement in over a week. The military base hospital transferred her to Sacred Heart Children's hospital where Zander had been a patient so many times before. The children's hospital performed various tests and even sent a scope into Arianna to take a look inside her intestines. After several days, the doctors decided that Arianna was fine and could go home. This was the last thing that Trisha wanted. It sent her into a state of panic.

She was in her element and did not want Arianna released. She insisted that the baby still had not had a bowel movement during the entire hospitalization. An intern talked with Trisha and questioned her about this. Trisha confirmed again that Arianna had not had a bowel movement during the entire hospitalization or the week leading up to that and added that she now was not urinating. This intern, this young brilliant intern, had a feeling that something was not right. She went into the bathroom and found two soiled diapers that proved her suspicions. Not wanting to arouse suspicion in Trisha, she said nothing and reported this to one of the other doctors. This doctor immediately contacted Florida Department of Children Services and Trisha was apprized of the situation. Social Services was sending a case worker to pick Arianna up and she would be discharged to a foster home.

Trisha called me crying hysterically letting me know of these accusations. Although I would like to tell you that I was now relieved and had the blinders removed from my eyes, I did not. I still believed her. I knew she had a history of lying, but once again, the actress in her was so convincing that I fell for it. If you have never been deceived at this level, you cannot truly understand how convincing an MBP abuser can be. Remember, she had fooled dozens of doctors for over three years now.

Before the social worker arrived at the hospital to pick up Arianna, Kevin called me to tell me that they had just arrived at his home and taken Zander as well. Kevin was devastated and I assured him that I would do everything in my power to help. Shortly after, Social Services arrived at the hospital to collect Arianna, but not before allowing Trisha to give her one last bottle. This was a big mistake. Arianna was discharged and placed with a foster family who immediately returned with her to the hospital because she was now experiencing tremors and jerks in her arms. She had not had this symptom during her entire hospitalization, but was now back at the hospital with a new symptom. This only made the doctors suspect Trisha more because she was the last one to feed Arianna a bottle.

I called that day and hired a lawyer. I had just found out that my two grandchildren were both in separate foster homes and that was all the information that I had. I still was not aware of all of the information that I now have and wanted to help my son get his children back. I called the Florida Department of Children and Families (DCF) office and talked with a very nice supervisor who assured me the children were fine. The next morning, Kevin and Trisha arrived in court to hear that the children would not be returned any time soon. Children's services started a case plan and Kevin and Trish did everything they were told. Although both children were never together and were moved at least three times each, their health was never an issue. Neither of the children were sick during this time.

PART 2
The Trials

CHAPTER 16

The Trial

The children were in foster care for about eight weeks. They were both moved several times and never placed together in the same home. While in foster care, their medical state was followed closely. Neither of them became sick nor had any kind of illness while away from their mother. Trisha and Kevin had complied with their case plan and eventually the children were returned home. It had been made very clear to them that any medical treatment would need to be reported to DCF immediately. The same day that the children were returned, Trisha stated that Zander was once again having seizures. He was taken to see a neurologist in Pensacola who admitted him to Sacred Heart Children's Hospital that evening. Trisha was desperate to convince everyone that Zander really was sick. She now had a neurologist that believed her. I could not believe the timing of his "seizure," and that it happened the very same day he was reunited with his mother. Apparently a lone social worker also "could not believe it."

It was April of 2008 and Arianna celebrated her second birthday at home with her parents. Kevin was planning to discharge from the military in just three months and they were making their plans to move back to California, however, they could not move home until DCF closed the open case. Although Kevin talked a lot about moving home, he said that Trisha now expressed that she did not want to leave "Mama" Tina.

Toward the end of April, Kevin and Trisha were informed that the Department of Children and Families had decided to take their case to a trial that would begin the third week of May. I was unsure what this meant, but their attorney asked me to fly out and testify. By now, the attorney had already collected $3,500 from me, and stated that he would need an additional $5,000 to go to trial. I felt I had no choice, but to give him a credit card. My grandchildren's lives were at stake. I wanted them out of Florida and home in California.

I flew out in May to be there for the trial. Kevin and Trisha had decided to go ahead and move out of base housing to collect the housing allowance for the last two months of Kevin's term. They were planning to rent a room from Tina. I helped them move their belongings into storage and rented a temporary room on base housing while I visited. The night before the trial, we were all very nervous and worried. I did not know what to expect. We sat and watched the season 7 finale of American Idol, the David Cook versus David Archuleta Finale. I had loved this show, but due to the circumstances, I was quite detached. I thought about how Trisha and I had watched that first season finale together and how much had changed since then.

We arrived at the court house just before eight in the morning as the attorney had requested. I was surprised when the attorney excluded me from the conversation between Kevin and Trisha. He did not have any problem talking with me about collecting money, but now he excluded me. All of the witnesses came and waited in the very small waiting room. It was as small as a doctor's office waiting room. Two of Zander's pediatricians from the military base had been subpoenaed. They both arrived in full dress uniform. They also had a military attorney present with them. One of the doctors was extremely nervous and it showed. Trisha tried to make conversation with them, but their attorney, as well as ours, discouraged it.

More and more witnesses arrived including Tina, several social workers, the intern, and the doctor from the children's hospital that had originally reported the suspected abuse. For the sake of the privacy of this doctor, I will call her Dr. Kay. There were two social workers whom I will refer to as Dee and Helen. Dee was assigned as the children's caseworker, and Helen was the worker that had followed her gut and insisted that this case go to trial. The tension in the waiting room was quite noticeable. There were just enough chairs for the people waiting so no one could sit leaving the comfort of an empty chair between them. I sat directly across from Dr. Kay and Trisha sat beside me. I watched as Trisha shot glaring looks at this doctor. Dr. Kay sat quietly and reviewed a stack of folders that she held. Kevin and Trisha were the first to be called into the court room. I looked around at the remaining potential witnesses. It seemed to be "us" verses "them," but I had no way of knowing who was "us" and who was "them."

I tried not to make much conversation, but people did talk. I talked to Dee about how we had gone to Destin Beach the day before and how different the white sands were compared to the beaches I had seen in California. We discussed the weather and I shared how I had now made several trips to Florida and did not care at all for the humidity. I watched as Dr. Kay kept reading over her documents. What could she have in those documents that could possibly justify taking my grandchildren from their parents? I tried to gauge her facial expressions. I was feeling some deep rooted anger toward this woman, but there was something about her, something genuine.

I was very nervous about testifying. I had previously worked as a State Employee, and was trying to recall the class I had taken on proper courtroom testimony protocol. I had worn a navy suit while most of the other witnesses, including our attorney, wore jeans. I felt a bit out of place and very hot. We waited in that waiting room for hours. Finally around half past twelve, they all came out and told us to go to lunch until two in the afternoon. I could not believe this had already gone on this long.

Trisha brought Tina along to lunch and the two kept talking in secretive tones. I was reflecting back on all the stories Trisha had told me about her mother. All the stories that I had learned were not true. God only knows what stories Trisha was telling Tina about me. I just wanted this case to be over, and Kevin, Trisha, and the kids to come home. I did not picture much beyond that. I just wanted those babies to come home.

We met back at the courthouse at the appointed time and again waited. I waited for several more hours. Finally, Trisha and the attorney came out and I thought it was over. The attorney told Tina she needed to go pick up the kids on base because the daycare closed at six in the evening, and they would not be able to make it on time. I gave Tina the money to pay the day care center and she left.

I had been waiting since eight in the morning and it was now after five in the afternoon. I was finally called in to testify. I was questioned about the dates and times of Zander's hospitalizations while he had lived in California. Not wanting to make a mistake, I asked the judge if estimated dates were okay. He said that was fine. I testified that I remembered four hospitalizations during the eight months Zander lived in my home. Then they asked me how many times Arianna was hospitalized while living in California. I explained that Arianna had never lived in California. They seemed confused and I explained when Zander and Trisha lived in California that Arianna had not yet been born. Hadn't this attorney done their homework? Then they asked if I ever personally saw Trisha harm Zander, and I said I had not. Finally, they asked me to explain some of Zander's health conditions. I remember starting to tell about the doctor he saw for his low weight and then my nerves got the best of me. Being as honest as I could be, I just froze and uttered "I… I just lost my train of thought." "Witness dismissed." That was it! I had waited nine hours to testify for five minutes about basically nothing. I was beating myself up later about the "I just lost my train of thought" comment. With everything I had ever been trained about court room testimony, I knew that credibility was what was most important. I felt I had just shown that I could not recall anything. I see now how easy it is to confuse a nervous witness.

After the conclusion of the day, we were instructed to come back first thing in the morning to quickly "finish up." We went back to the temporary housing on base. The kids were tired and went to bed pretty early. We were all exhausted and emotionally drained. We were anxious for court the next day hoping the judge would wrap this up and allow Kevin and Trisha to move back to California with the children. I had been praying a lot, but still did not feel a peace about the situation. I wasn't sure why.

The next morning, we arrived back at the courthouse. It had not been even a half hour before Trisha came out screaming.

She looked at me and said, "Mom, they are taking my kids!"

I was in shock. I had no idea what could have happened in the court room the previous day, but I did not expect this. For a brief second, a very brief second, I thought about getting my grandkids, jumping in my rental car, and driving away with them. I would drive away and not stop until we arrived in California. No one had told me that I could not take them anywhere. Although my heart wanted to do this, my common sense kicked in and told me not to. It was then that I asked Kevin and Trisha, "If they will not give the kids to you, do you care if I ask for them to give them to me." They both simultaneously stated an agreeable "yes." That was it. I had a plan.

CHAPTER 17

Waving Goodbye

We had been back on base less then thirty minutes when Helen called and said they would be there any minute and to have Zander's medication and the kids clothes packed. Trisha went nuts! She started grabbing Zander's medication saying, "Mom, Mom, help me count these. They are going to know how many he has taken."

I was still in shock and had no clue what she meant. While I was packing the kids clothing and hugging and kissing them, Trisha was in the kitchen counting Zander's pills and dumping some of them down the sink. I still do not fully understand what that was about. I can only assume that she had not been giving him his seizure medications because she was the only one who knew that he did not need them.

Helen and another case worker arrived. They had a military security escort with them. I tried with everything I had to hold myself together but could not. Through tears, I pleaded with Helen, "Tell me what you want? Tell me what I need to do? I will do it. I love those babies so much, just tell me what you want me to do and I will do it. Please just give them to me."

Helen actually appeared to have compassion when she responded, "We are working on that."

That was all that she said. I watched as Zander waved "good-bye" to us like he thought he was going on a fun outing. Arianna just followed what her brother was doing saying "bye-bye." They drove away as Trisha fumed, Kevin was in disbelief and I just stood crying.

"What just happened?"

The military police had the presence of mind to recognize our grief and arranged for a chaplain to come and counsel with us. When he arrived, I was very receiving. Trisha had not cried once until the Chaplain arrived and then she put on an amazing performance. She even added shivering and sobbing while burying her face in her hands. I had seen this before when she had sat on my couch so many years before telling me about the awful things that had happened to her. I had seen this act before. I was tired of it.

Later that day, Trisha displayed what I remember as very bizarre behavior. Kevin and I were grieving. Out of nowhere, Trisha demanded "I want to go out to dinner." I was in no mood to go out to eat and retreated to my bedroom. I could hear Kevin telling Trisha they did not have the money to go out. He was hurting too. His kids had just been ripped from him hours before. Trisha continued to insist and tantrum that she wanted to go out to eat. She came pounding on my door demanding we go out to eat and just continually whined that she was hungry. I was not in the mood for it, and told her to go make a sandwich. She started yelling at me and calling me horrible names. She called me every name and curse word imaginable because I would not jump up and take her out to dinner. Her screaming went on for some time.

I could hear her pleading with Kevin, like a child that keeps insisting when you tell them "no." She cried like a baby and said over and over that she was hungry and wanted McDonald's. Kevin finally told her to go apologize to me for the names she called me and he would take her. She cried out "No" screaming "I'm hungry!" Then she pleaded with him not to make her apologize. This went on for some time when she finally crept down the hall and knocked on my door. "Mama" I hear from the other side of the door, using her fake baby talk. She was sounding like the same little girl that had sat on my couch years earlier and told me all the made up stories for attention.

She opened my door and said, "Mama, I sorry mama."

I acknowledged her apology and she began dancing in my room singing the kids song "if you're happy and you know it clap your hands." Again, she was singing like a baby. It was a pathetic display. Once again, she was trying to demand attention just hours after the children had been taken from us. Watching her shift from viscous attack to tantruming child to baby talk was like watching a scene from the movie *Sybil*.

Two days later, DCF called and told us that we would be allowed to visit Arianna. We were told that Zander was placed back in his previous foster home, in another city, that was more equipped to handle his "medical issues." Arianna's foster parents had agreed to meet us at a public park. They brought lunch and tried to make it a very nice visit for us. The couple, Jennifer and Jason, had three teenage girls. The girls seemed to really enjoy Arianna. The family was compassionate and kind. I spent most of my time playing with Arianna in the play area. Trisha spent the entire visit talking to the family. She told stories about how sick Zander was and how frightened she was when he was airlifted on the helicopter. She said that, at one point while in the hospital, she thought Zander was going to pass away. Hearing her talk about this just sickened me. She had shown no emotion at all when Zander was sick. The only feeling she had shown was satisfaction. Even now, when she should be visiting with Arianna, she was making this visit all about her. She had a brand-new stage with a fresh and captive audience.

When we said our "goodbyes" to Arianna, she ran over and hugged me. She kept saying "car" and pointing to my car. I told her "no baby" that she could not go with me. Then, in all of her beautiful innocence, she said "don't cry." They buckled her into the car seat and began to drive away. She waved at me as she left. This time I held back the tears. I watched as her pretty smile and little blonde curls faded into the distance.

CHAPTER 18

Again We Wait

Our attorney notified us that the next hearing date would be four weeks away and he wanted me present. We ended up staying the entire four weeks in temporary base housing. I should have flown home and come back for the hearing, but Kevin and Trisha now had no where to live so I stayed to rent the housing for them. This was proving to be quite costly. The attorney asked for another $3,500, and once again I handed him my credit card. He said he wanted to have Trisha see a psychiatrist who would testify on her behalf. The psychiatrist would cost another $2,000.

We were able to see Arianna several more times. Finally, after more than two weeks, a visit with Zander was arranged. We were to meet him at a visiting facility half way between the base and the home he was in. When Zander arrived, he was not himself. His foster mother explained that "Alex" was now on some new medications that make him a bit groggy. We corrected her and told her that we call him Zander not Alex. She continued to refer to him as Alex several more times during the visit. Afterwards, I mentioned to Dee, the case worker, that we did not like the way Zander seemed to be over medicated. He was normally an active and hyper somewhat behaviorally challenged little boy, but this day, he just seemed lost in a daze. Dee said she would look into it.

It was late June 2008, and the next hearing date had arrived. This time, it was an open court and all the witnesses were allowed in the court room. Kevin and Trisha sat in front with their attorney and I sat behind them. Jennifer, Arianna's foster mother, was also in attendance. The judge mostly talked back and forth with counsel asking questions of both sides. He asked if the children had been ill or had any hospitalizations while in foster care. They had not. The judge said a few things that I had not heard before. He repeated what Dr. Kay had said in her testimony. He said, "This doctor sat in my court room and stated she was one hundred percent positive that this woman had Munchausen by proxy... This doctor said she knew that this mother was doing this to the children and she would stake her medical license on that diagnosis. I must tell you that I have never had a doctor sit in my court room and tell me they are one hundred percent positive of anything before. I am inclined to believe her testimony."

He also mentioned that Dr. Kay said that she had to protect these children as they "had no voice" and she had to be their "voice." The judge asked about the status of the Interstate Compact Placement. The caseworkers stated they are in process of working through Tallahassee to contact Sacramento to approve the Interstate Compact. Up to this point, I was not sure what they were talking about. The judge asked "is the grandmother here?" I answered him. He asked me if I was willing to take on the responsibility of the children and I agreed. He went on to say "that is quite a responsibility." I told him that my grandchildren were my life. He then told the caseworkers to move forward with the process to get California's approval to accept the children. They were actually trying to get the children to me. I was so overjoyed and relieved.

Dee told me that an interstate compact placement agreement (ICPC) could take months to approve and it would not be any time soon. Just knowing they were working on it was enough for me.

It was explained to me that had I lived in the same state the children would have been placed with me prior to being placed in foster care. Transferring children from one state to another would take the county forwarding the case to Florida's state capital, Tallahassee and then being forwarded to California's state capital, Sacramento. From there, it would be sent to my local county and then my local child services would open a case and do a home study of my home. Although I was the children's grandmother, I was still going to have to do a great deal of work on my end to get the children placed in my home.

I mentioned to Jennifer I would be flying back home to California the following day, and she offered to let me come to her home to visit Arianna before I left. I visited Arianna that evening and brought her a bag full of new clothes, hair bows, and some toys. In the month, I was there I was only able to see Zander that one time.

CHAPTER 19

Going Home Alone

Because I had previously considered adopting a child several years earlier, I was a bit familiar with the expectations of a placement home study. I decided to stay one step ahead of Florida's requests. As soon as I returned home, I enrolled in my county's nine-week foster care classes, and also updated my first aid and CPR certification. While taking these classes, during this time, I was provided a form to have a physical from my doctor which I followed through with. Doing these things without being asked to do them proved to be a gesture that I was serious. There was, however, one dark cloud in completing my home study. Three months before the children were placed in foster care, my husband and I separated and were seeking a divorce. I did not want the details of this made public, but in the spirit of full disclosure, I had to disclose it. My husband did step up and help me with every detail along the way as well as getting my home child proofed and ready for the children.

July came and Kevin was discharged from the Air Force; however, he was not able to leave Florida while his kids were in foster care. It was a hard time because all he wanted to do is come back home with his children. Kevin and Trisha's belongings were shipped to my home and stored in my garage.

It seemed as if we had another hearing date every three to four weeks. I would be ready to testify by phone and would wait for the phone to ring. Each and every time I would get a call that nothing had been decided and we would have yet another hearing date another month away. It was now early August and a lot had changed. Trisha had decided that she was not returning to California. She and Kevin had moved in with Tina, and Kevin had to decide what to do. He eventually decided to file for divorce and I helped him with that. Kevin decided to stay with a friend while waiting the outcome of this case. Trisha decided to stay with her "Mama" Tina who would soon be moving to Mobile, Alabama. Trisha eventually went with her to Alabama. She also found a new boyfriend in Alabama and began to groom his mother as her *next* "Mama."

It was during this time I saw even more of Trisha's true evil side. She would do and say anything to keep the children from coming to me. She had told her new attorney (because I stopped paying for the other one) that I was a drug addict, drug dealer, and emotionally and physically unstable. I am not sure if anyone believed her, but when Dee told me that she said this in the last hearing I was shocked. As soon as Dee asked me about my health, I told her I recently had an adoption physical and was taking foster care classes. I provided her my physical along with blood tests to counter Trisha's ridiculous claim.

Trisha had said something else about me that truly shook me to my core. She told her attorney and psychiatrist that the reason I was getting a divorce was because I had an abortion behind my husband's back and that it was not his. She also stated that she had accompanied me to the abortion. Although I was unsure if anyone actually believed this, I had to open up and share that not only did I struggle for years with infertility and the grief of not having more children, but that I had a hysterectomy several years before meeting Trisha, so her claims were once again ludicrous. Trisha knew that my own

76

infertility was one of my biggest heartbreaks. I have no doubt this accusation was calculated intentionally because she knew how much it would hurt me. Trisha had sunk to a whole new low with this accusation. Her sole intention was to hurt and destroy my character. I remembered Trisha's mothers last words to me, "Tammy, watch out. She will turn on you. She will try to destroy you." What a prophet her mother was.

Trisha stated in one of the hearings that the kids do not even know me and had no contact with me. Jennifer happened to be in that hearing and spoke up telling the judge that I called Arianna all the time and had sent her several packages with clothing as well as money to buy her other things. I was so thankful for Jennifer during this time. Jennifer was instrumental in helping me see the rainbow at the end of this heartbreak. I was so thankful that Arianna was with a family that loved her and allowed me to have a relationship with her. I was not allowed this with Zander's foster family.

CHAPTER 20

The Pieces Come Together

It was early fall and my seasonal allergies had begun. I had been sick for a few weeks with a bad case of bronchitis. When I needed to use my Albuterol inhaler I noticed it said to repeat a second time if symptoms do not improve. A few minutes later, I took a second puff of the inhaler. Shortly after the second dose my arms started to jerk. It was like a nervous jerk that I just had to shake them. Suddenly, a flood of memory came to me of the day Trisha had told me to look at Zander, that he was having a seizure when his arms were jerking. I was having the same arm jerking after taking my second dose of Albuterol.

It was not until that moment that I instantly realized that she had given Zander liquid Albuterol to make his arms jerk so that it would appear as if he was having a seizure. Then I remembered how Trisha had given Arianna her last bottle in the hospital, and her foster parents immediately returned her to the hospital with arm jerking. I had remembered seeing some medications of Zander's in the boxes of their belongings in my garage. I ran outside and found the box. It was liquid Albuterol.

Dee had mentioned to Kevin that they had thought Trisha had put something in Arianna's bottle at the hospital that day, but they did not test the bottle so could not prove it. Kevin had mentioned that Trisha always kept the Albuterol in the diaper bag. It was not until this moment that all the puzzle pieces seemed to fit. It all came together and I realized that everything she was accused of doing was true. Up to this point, I had been praying for God to open my eyes and clearly show me the truth. I honestly believe this was an answer to my prayers.

My eyes were fully open for the first time. My Trisha blinders had been removed. I seemed to go through all five stages of grief in the days to follow. I now knew what I had to do. I had to fight Trisha head on to protect these children. I had to be their voice. "Their voice," that is what Dr. Kay had said in her testimony. I reflected on my feelings in the court waiting room staring down this doctor that I first resented, but now owed everything. The doctor that said "These children do not have a voice. I have to be their voice." Oh thank you, God, that she was their voice when I was not. I had not yet found my voice.

It was with great humility that I decided to make the phone call to Trisha's mother. The mother who adopted her at age eight. I reiterate the adoption only because the family does not want it to appear that they had anything to do with causing Trisha to become such a broken person. She was very emotionally troubled when she came to live with them. Her mother had warned me that Trisha would turn on me. When she answered the phone, she was the same graceful kind hearted woman that I remembered. She had not had contact with Trisha since that evening in my living room where she confronted her lies. She did not want contact with her either. She did however, want to help save these children from Trisha. She shared a great deal of information. She even reminded me that she had previously told me to look for signs of MBP before Trisha ever had children. At the time, I did not even know what MBP was. With her prompting, I did recall the warning. This made me a bit angry with myself.

It was this same week that I called and spoke to Helen. Helen was the social worker that followed her gut to bring this case to trial. I already knew they were concerned about giving the children to a relative that had believed and unknowingly enabled Trisha. I told Helen that I had come to the realization that Trisha had been the one making the children sick. I told her how I put things together to finally see the truth. I also gave her Trisha's mother's phone number whom she was very eager to talk to. It was all coming together.

I stayed in constant contact with Jennifer, Arianna's foster mother. She let me call and talk to Arianna anytime I wanted to. I continued to send her new clothes and she would share photos and videos of some of the fun things Arianna was doing. It was a completely different experience with Zander's foster family. I had only visited with him once since all this happened. When his fourth birthday came in July, I was not allowed to call him. I was not able to send a gift or even a card. This broke my heart! I did see a video of his Birthday celebration posted on Trisha's MySpace account. It was a small way to see that he was okay. His foster family had bought him a yellow dump truck, and there was a video of Arianna pushing him around in the dump truck. I probably watched that video fifty times. It was all I had.

During the next three months, there were a few more court hearings. Dee was in constant contact with me asking for multiple documents to get my home study cleared. The paperwork was end-less. One day, while discussing with Dee that Trisha was now wanting to stay in Florida with Tina, she corrected me and said, "you mean her Mom." I told her that Tina was not her Mom, but a woman they met on the Air Force base. She was baffled as she told me that Trisha told her that was her mother, her actual mother and that was why Tina was allowed on all of the visits with the children. I think Dee too was finally figuring out that most of what Trisha said was a lie. All the caseworkers were starting to catch Trisha in more and more lies.

When Helen was talking to Trisha's mother she was stunned to find out Trisha had never been in an auto accident that resulted in her limp and the scars on her neck and back. She had been telling that story to them for months. Trisha had also begun a trail of behavior that did not help case her at all. During this time, she was arrested and charged with shoplifting. She also began writing checks on her and Kevin's previous closed bank accounts and a warrant was issued for her arrest. She had already moved to Alabama, but when she arrived for one of the custody hearings she was arrested at the court house.

We had one court date after another. Each and every time I would get my heart set on bringing the kids home. I would be so disappointed when they told me nothing was settled and they would meet again in four weeks. Finally, that November, it happened. Jennifer called me even before the case worker did.

"Guess who is coming to California?" she exclaimed.

I burst out with joy and Jennifer burst into tears.

"I wanted this for you. I wanted this for Arianna, but I did not realize it would hurt this much," she said.

Arianna had now been with her family for six months and they loved her very much. Jennifer had done exactly what I had been taught to do in the Foster Care classes I had taken. She was being a bridge between Arianna and her family, no matter how much it hurt her. What a completely different experience than I had with Zander's foster family. Suddenly, I realized the date, November 4, 2008. It was that same day Barack Obama won the Presidential Election. Although I had not voted for him, I found myself not really caring about the election. I had everything that I had prayed for.

PART 3

The Triumph

How Tragedy + Trials + Time = Triumph

CHAPTER 21

At Last

It took a little over a week to get a reasonably priced flight to Florida as well as the children's one way flights home. I flew into New Orleans and rented a car to drive into Fort Walton Beach. Jennifer and her family had graciously offered to allow me to stay with them during my trip. With Arianna being only two and a half years old, I thought she would need an adjustment period to reacquaint with me before leaving Jennifer and her family. She had been with them for six months and had not seen me in just as long.

Jennifer had made sure that Arianna did not forget me. She had been telling her that Grandma was going to take her to live in California. When I arrived at Jennifer's house, Arianna ran out to me saying, "Grandma, we are going to California," then she said, "go get my Bubba right now."

I spent a total of four nights with Jennifer. The first two days I spent with Arianna, and after two days I drove to the city where Zander was living to pick him up.

Dee had already provided me with a copy of the court order. I arranged a time to arrive at the home where Zander had been living for the last six months. Kevin went along with me to pick him up. I had already read some of Libby, the foster mother's, posts on MySpace. She was not at all happy that I was getting custody of

Zander. She had written a comment on her page that said "the judge has decided that 'Alex' will be going to California to live with his grandmother." Several of her friends and relatives wrote comments about how horrible it was and that the judge had no sense at all. They wrote that "Alex" should stay in Florida with his "family" that loved him. It frustrated me to read because I *was* his family and I *did* love him. I loved him more than any of them could even imagine.

When I arrived at their home, Libby met me in the front yard. I greeted her and asked how she was doing. She responded, "I'm a mess," she went on to say, "I don't think Alex should be going to California. I think he should live *here* with people who love him and can take care of him."

Well how nice for you. His name is not Alex, I thought to myself, but never said out loud. I knew in my heart she was lashing out in pain, pain she had for the love of a child, for the love of my Zander. This was the kind of love his "mother" had never felt for him. I knew all too well what that pain felt like. I felt compassion for this woman rather than anger.

She said, "I heard you are going to take him off all of his medications. Alex is doing really well on his medications."

"I bet! Let's drug him into a stupor so he is easier to take care of."

I didn't say that out loud either, but quietly kept my responses in my head.

Libby invited us into the house where her daughter and Zander sat at the table eating French toast. She said, "Alex needs to finish his breakfast before he leaves."

Zander, now four years old, was wearing cable braces on his legs to help straighten them. This was to correct the leg that was turned in when he was born. She showed me how his braces went on and then sat down at the kitchen table and began to go over his school and medical records. She showed me his medications and explained the dosage. He was now on five different medications. Over and over, she kept referring to him as Alex while we continued to call him Zander, which he no longer responded to. At this point. I was feeling as if every time she said the name "Alex" she was being passive aggressive trying to claim ownership. She *knew* he had always been called Zander. What right did she have to change his name?

Several of Libby's family members, including her parents, were there to say "goodbye." They all hugged him and took some last photos with him. They walked with us out to the car. Libby made another comment about how she did not think it was right that I was taking him out of Florida.

I looked over at Libby's mother and said, "If this was your grandchild," pointing to her granddaughter, "what would you do?"

"The same thing," she responded.

We said one last "goodbye" and drove away. As we left, I saw Libby cry as Zander waved "goodbye." My thoughts went back to that day six months earlier when Zander waved "goodbye" to me as he was taken away by the social workers. Once again, I felt a great deal of compassion for what this family must be feeling. It had to be hard to have a child live in your home for six months and then have him leave. I thought of the story in the Bible in the book of 1 Kings. The story where two women were claiming to be the mother of the same baby. To find out which was the true mother King Solomon said to cut the baby in half. The true mother quickly spoke up saying "no" and agreed to let the other mother have the child. This was how Solomon knew which one was the true mother. I was sure glad I did not have to go through that test to prove my love for Zander. Trisha, who wanted Zander to remain in Florida in foster care, would have no problem cutting him in half, as long as she got attention and sympathy for doing so.

Zander and I arrived at Jennifer's house. Arianna came running outside to see her brother. She screamed "Bubba" and ran to him.

During the six months, they were in foster care they were only able to see each other once a month. They had missed each other tremendously. This was a happy reunion. Zander was happy, but he was also confused. The medications caused him to stare off into space. When the medication wore off, he was an angry, hyperactive, out of control fit to be reckoned. I knew I had to find a middle ground if I was ever going to be able to help Zander heal.

Finally Back Together

Sibling Love

CHAPTER 22

The Goodbye Visit

The next day, I was told to take the kids to meet Dee and Trisha at a nearby McDonald's for their final visit. Trisha had brought Tina and they played with the kids for about an hour. Trisha kept referring to Tina as "Grandma" to the kids. I hated that. I noticed a police car stayed parked in the parking lot the entire time we were there. He was still parked there when we left. I do not know if this was requested by children's services, but I suspected so. When it was time to walk out to my car, Trisha was holding Arianna's hand.

Arianna pulled away and said, "Mommy, I do not want to hold your hand, I want to hold Grandma's hand."

I put Arianna in the car and turned back around to get Zander from Trisha's arms.

I heard Trisha cry out to Tina saying, "Mama, they took my baby" while reaching for her arms of sympathy.

Only this time, when she cried out "they took my baby," she was not referring to her dog.

"Just let him go, Trisha, it's not over," Tina told her.

She called out again to Tina "Mama" she cried hysterically.

I thought to myself, *She's all yours now, Tina. I have everything that matters.*

Arianna, Zander, and I spent two more days with Jennifer and her family. They were sad to see Arianna leave. Each of Jennifer's daughters said their personal "goodbyes" before leaving for school. I was very moved when I watched Jennifer's oldest daughter say her final goodbye and just walk away in tears. This was heartbreaking, but I was so thankful that Arianna had been loved so very much. I had suggested that Jennifer have her three girls write a letter to Arianna that I could keep for her when she was older. All three of them did. Jennifer also gave me a photo album full of photos they had taken of Arianna. This was a true blessing.

CHAPTER 23

The Moment I Had Been Praying For

Was this really happening? I had prayed for this day for so long. The day had finally come that we could all leave Florida. The three of us packed up the rental car and headed to New Orleans. We spent one night in New Orleans and took a shuttle to the airport the next morning. I got a lot of looks because I used two of those animal back pack harnesses with a strap and handle to hold onto the children. I am usually not a fan of those "children leashes," but let me explain: three suitcases, one purse, one diaper bag, one carry on with toys and snacks, and two hyperactive children's hands. Children who had no idea where this "Grandma lady" was taking them and each wanting their perspective foster mothers. It was not going to go well! Besides, they loved their "monkey packs" even if I got multiple scorning looks from other disapproving mothers. Although I did not know it yet, I would have to learn to get used to unapproving looks from strangers.

While walking down the terminal to the gate, Zander stopped at the very first plane we saw. He wanted on that plane and he wanted on that plane now. He did not understand that we had to walk quite a long way down to our plane. He threw himself to the ground yanking on my wrist in protest. It sprained my wrist. It took a lot of coaching and explaining to get him to finally get up and move on down the terminal. We saw several more planes before we arrived at our gate. He repeated his loud protest with each plane we passed. Finally, we arrived at our gate, however, it was not quite time for our plane to board. There were two other planes arriving at the gate before ours would arrive. Each plane sending Zander into a raging tantrum.

Zander was not having any of it. He was completely obsessed with getting on that plane. Although he was now four years old, he still did not speak. He only made grunts and sounds and a few jumbled words that I did not understand. I sat on the floor face to face with him and tried to communicate to him what was happening. In return, he spit in my face, not exactly the communication I had wanted. I got a few of those *looks* from people. One man wearing a yellow shirt mumbled under his breath while giving me an eye roll. I didn't care what he thought. I cared about what this baby was thinking. He could not tell me. He had spent the first three years of his life in and out of the hospital, being poisoned by this mother, and then the last year in multiple foster homes separated from his sister. Finally, he was in one home for six months, started to call another woman "Mama" and then I came along and took him away from his safe place. This was Zander's reality. He did not even know that he was Zander. He thought he was Alex.

Eventually, our plane arrived and both of the children were thrilled to board. The man in the yellow shirt was seated across the isle and up a few rows from us during the first leg of the flight. Fortunately for him, Southwest has an open seating plan. He was less than amused by the children standing up, sitting down, standing up again, crying, screaming, messing with the air vents, turning the lights on and off, sitting down, throwing toys, and throwing goldfish and crayons. When the plane landed in Phoenix, the man could not move his seat fast enough while he once again mumbled under his breath. Zander was in full tantrum mode when we landed and he realized we were not getting off the plane.

"Next stop," I told him, "Next stop."

The captain had to make a liar out of me by making an unplanned stop in Burbank.

"Oh, I mean next stop," as the tantrum went on, "next stop."

When we landed in Sacramento, I tried to scoot the kids along to the baggage claim. Zander was repeating his earlier behavior of throwing himself on the floor while yanking on my wrist. The man in the yellow shirt walked past us and shot me one last judging look. Zander threw himself on the terminal floor once again yanking on my wrist. I kept trying to reason with him, while dropping one bag after another, picking him up while trying to shuffle all of my bags as well as his sister who wanted to be carried. I felt like falling on the floor in a fit myself. Finally, a wonderful young woman came over and asked if she could help carry something while I tended to Zander. She was a lifesaver. She walked with me all the way to baggage claim and I told her a bit about our situation and how the kids were coming to live with me. She said she would pray for us and I thanked her.

We were finally home. All of us exhausted. I now had what I had worked and prayed so hard for. It had been eleven months since this ordeal began. Eleven long months since the kids were first placed in foster care, now they were home. I had their toddler beds set up and put them into bed. For so many months, I had walked into this empty bedroom and prayed for the day the children would be able to sleep here. I tucked them in their beds and stayed in the room until both of them fell asleep. It took well over an hour for them to fall asleep. I said one last prayer of thanks to God and went to sleep myself.

I had not been asleep more than an hour before I heard Zander barge into my room and crawl into my bed. His sister quickly followed. I waited for them to fall back asleep and carried them each back to their own beds. I did not want to start a habit of them wanting to sleep in my room. Two more times throughout the night, they each came and ended up back in my bed. Each time I waited until they fell back asleep and put them into their own beds. It happened one last time when I awoke to find them both sleeping next to me. I gave up and left them there until morning. I was just too tired to try to set this boundary tonight.

Because Zander had a problem with wandering out of his home on the air base, we had put motion alarms on the front door as well as his bedroom door. If he opened either door, the alarm would sound. After three nights of the alarm going off each and every time he got up to crawl in bed with me, I shut the bedroom alarm off and just left my door open. Each and every night, I would put them to bed in their own beds. Each and every morning, I would wake up with them both sleeping next to me. I finally resolved to myself that they needed this. They needed to be able to come to me when they woke up scared.

One night, Zander crawled in with me and said, "Mmm uh."

His sister quickly interpreted, "He wants his Mama," she then said, "I want my Mama too."

They were not talking about Trisha. Zander wanted Libby, and Arianna wanted Jennifer. How was I going to fix that?

CHAPTER 24

Finding Our New Normal

Although they were out of Florida, we still had our share of hurricanes. These children came to me very broken little souls. Zander's sadness manifested in anger. He threw everything he could throw. He slammed over coffee tables, dining room chairs, and lamps. He threw dishes across the room. Anything within his reach that he could lift he would throw. He would turn entire bookshelves over dumping books everywhere and then throw the books. I very quickly learned to empty all of the shelves and put all objects out of reach. He would even walk to the sink and pull the entire rack of dishes to the floor. He was mad! He was mad and he wanted me to know it. It did not help that he was unable to talk or communicate with me. His only form of communication was throwing things, and hitting, slapping, biting, pulling my hair, or spitting on me.

There was not a day that went by that he did not slam a lamp or dining chair over at least ten times. I put my nice dining chairs out in the garage, and brought Kevin and Trisha's beat up chairs into the house. I also could not get him to sit at the dinner table. He would come to the table and throw his plate of food across the room. His sister would copy him and throw her plate as well. I counted one evening that I picked up five plates of food between the two of them. I learned rather quickly not to put a full plate of food out but put two bites at a time on his plate. He would go throw a lamp then come take a bite. My goal at this time was to get him to eat one bite at a time. Over time, I learned how to help him with his anger, one thrown object at a time.

One day, it occurred to me that I needed to show him *how* to be mad. I had a Nerf ball and showed him how to throw it to the ground. I threw the ball to the ground and said, "I'm mad," while stomping my foot. He copied me. He stomped his foot while throwing the ball and mumbled a sound that somewhat resembled "mad." We did it again. "I'm mad" throwing the ball to the ground and stomping the foot. I was reaching him.

I gave him a few Nerf balls and told him, "When you are mad, this is what you throw."

The next time he knocked over a chair, I quickly grabbed the Nerf ball and said, "What do we do when we are mad?"

He threw the ball, stomped his foot, and giggled. Finally, he had a way to communicate to me that he was mad. Little by little over time, over several months, he stopped throwing over furniture. I later learned, while taking a behavioral modification class, that this was a method called replacement behavior. You give the child a replacement for the behavior you wish to extinguish.

Arianna was now two and a half years old and her hurt was in the form of insecurity. She did not want to be left alone anywhere. Multiple times a day, she would say, "Don't leave me," or "Grandma, don't go away." I could not walk into the bathroom without her crying out, "Don't leave me." Zander would fall asleep earlier in the evening so I would spend this time one on one with Arianna. I would sit and hold her in the rocking chair every night until she fell asleep. Sometimes, I would sit for two hours rocking her while praying or singing to her. She would open her eyes every few minutes to make sure she could still see me and that I was still holding her. When I carried her to bed and tucked her in she would look up in a panic to make sure I was still there. I had to stay next to her bed until she, was completely asleep.

2008

Several times during the day, I would find Arianna underneath the kitchen table hiding. She would crawl under the table and just curl into a ball. She would crawl under desks as well as curl up in the corner in the dog's bed. I extinguished this behavior by getting her a small colorful tent to play in. I let her take her dolls and blankets in there and would take her into her special place where she felt "safe." I would read to her in her tent and eventually she stopped hiding and began to heal.

Christmas 2009

Arianna called me "Grandma," but one day out of nowhere, she started calling me "Mama." Not wanting her to be confused, I reminded her that I was "Grandma." I did not want her to some day be surprised and think, *What you are not my real mother?* I wanted her to know that I was Grandma. When she continued to call me "Mama," I corrected her again saying, "Arianna, you know that I am your Grandma."

She looked up at me, with her big beautiful blue eyes staring right into mine, and said, "But… I have to call *someone* Mama."

My heart just sank. Yes, she did. She did have to call some-one Mama. I never corrected her again. From this moment on I was her Mama. Her brother quickly followed her lead and I became his Mama as well.

The days were long and the children needed attention and redirection every minute of every day. They were both very hyperactive and had continual behavioral issues. It was exhausting. Without the help of God, I do not know how I would have gotten through it. There were several times a day I would just throw my hands up in the air and ask God to help me carry this. My husband was becoming more and more helpful with the children. This was a good thing for us. We were taking the problems we had in our relationship and setting them aside to focus on what was best for these children. We started praying together and now had a common goal. God used even our tragedy to bring something good to our home.

Kevin was finally able to move back to California. He was visiting the children as often as he could when he was not working. My court order did say, however, that he could not live in my home. This was hard for all of us, but it helped Kevin to readjust after returning to civilian life. He had some anxiety to work through after his time in the Iraq war. He had healing of his own to focus on.

I took both children to see a pediatrician. I was hoping to address all of the medications Zander was taking and see if we could discontinue some of them. Florida DCF had made it very clear that I must not change or discontinue any of his medications without a doctor's supervision. They were definitely the most hyper and behaviorally challenged children in the waiting room. Arianna was quickly learning to copy her brother's behavior. At one point, Zander got so out of control that I had to put him on my lap and completely restrain him with both of my arms wrapped tightly around him. He did not like this at all and bit me in the upper arm so hard that it broke the skin. It was purple within seconds. Parents around the waiting room were giving me the looks that we so often got. I was getting used to the looks but it did not make it any easier.

The time came to finally see the pediatrician. Dr. Lester was welcoming and understanding. I told her about our situation and that the kids mother had MBP. I told her that I had no idea how much of Zander's medical records were accurate, and how much was his mothers exaggerated or false medical history. I had already read several things in his medical records where his mother had lied about his health history. I handed the doctor about a six inch stack of medical and school documents on Zander as well as a court order. She had it all photocopied. She was amazing! She started by taking the time to praise me for what I was doing. Then she calmly told me that we were going to "start from scratch" with Zander's medical history.

The first thing she did was take a look at his leg braces that attached to his shoes and said, "Who gave him those?"

I explained that they were ordered by a doctor in Florida while he was in foster care. She said they do not work, and she has not known of a doctor that has prescribed them in over twenty years. It was becoming evident that a lot of the things "prescribed" to Zander while in foster care seemed to be a doctor's way of getting medical payments. She took a look at each of Zander's prescriptions. He was on medications for asthma, seizures, mood stabilizers, and two different medications for attention deficit disorder. Dr. Lester referred me to a specialist for neurology, orthopedics, allergies, and psychiatry. I have to praise this doctor because between this appointment and my follow up appointment, she had reviewed every document I had given her. Zander started out on five medications. Over time, I had one specialist at a time take him off several of the medications until he was finally only on two.

Because I had only temporary guardianship and still had to comply with caseworkers in both Florida and California, I had to report to Dee once a week and a case worker came to my home every other week. Florida had retained jurisdiction on the case. Trisha still had an attorney and filed multiple motions to have the children returned to Florida. She had a plan. She had asked Libby to have her home approved for one more foster child. She then filed a motion to have both children returned to Florida hoping to have them both placed in Libby's home. This worried me, but when the hearings came up the judge declined her multiple requests. The caseworker told the judge that the children were thriving and should stay with me.

It was a challenge to take the children anywhere. Zander's behavior was so bad that I found it difficult to do anything outside the home. He had a new behavior where he would unbuckle his car seat as soon as I started driving. I would pull over buckle him back in and he would repeat this multiple times. Sometimes he unbuckled himself and then unbuckled his sister as well. By the time I arrived at my destination I had pulled over six or seven times. One day while in the checkout line at Wal-Mart, Zander was sitting inside the cart while I had his sister sitting in the front of the cart. He kept throwing items out of the cart onto the floor. I would pick them up and tell him to stop.

He did this multiple times and would laugh and hit my hand when I put them back in. Finally I just held on to his hands trying to get him to stop. He let out an intensely loud scream. He was out of control. A man in line who had already given me many looks turned back and yelled at me, "Can't you control your kid?"

In total frustration I responded back, "No, sir, actually, I cannot! Were you offering to help because I could use a break now and then? Are you available on Tuesday?"

He shut up. Everyone in line laughed. I felt bad because I became sarcastic to a total stranger. I am usually pretty good at biting my tongue and only thinking a smart remark, but this time I was a bit worn down and fell prey to the ugly temptation to justify myself. I should not have said that, but I wonder if he thought twice before ever lashing out at another over-stressed mother. If so, then it was worth it.

Although Zander's special needs had not yet been diagnosed, he was still non-verbal and acted out a lot. It had been suggested by a doctor in Florida that he was autistic. At times, when he acted out in public and I felt a need to explain I would just say, "he is autistic" or "he does not understand." It made the looks and what I perceived as judgment easier to bear if I explained his behavior. People seem to understand if they see a reason behind the behavior.

CHAPTER 25

School Starts

Next came getting Zander enrolled in school. Children with language or speech delays are eligible to start school at three years old. Zander was four so he was enrolled in pre-school. When I read Zander's IEP (Individual Education Plan) from the preschool he attended in Florida, I noticed one of his goals was for "Alex" to learn to respond to his own name. This just made me more frustrated with Libby. Of course he did not respond to "Alex." No one had ever called him that. Part of me understood Libby's motivation. When I had taken the foster care classes, there were so many people becoming foster parents for the purpose of adoption. Several couples shared how they had previously adopted, but not before having multiple foster children come and go from their home. They had to wait until one of those children were available to adopt due to family members unable or unwilling to care for them. I know she loved him and was hoping to adopt him, but Zander was not available to adopt. He was wanted and he was loved by *his* family.

Although I now had the children, I was still required to allow Trisha phone calls with them. Trisha called at all hours of the day; and if I did not answer the phone each and every time, she reported to Dee that I was refusing her calls. Even before I had left Florida with the kids, I knew the phone call thing was a problem. At Trisha's goodbye visit, I had told her that we were going to New Orleans the following day, would spend the night, and then fly home the next day. I told her we would be flying all day long and I would call her the day after I arrived in California. She probably left me ten voice mail messages on the day we were flying home. I had told her I would be unavailable to take her calls that day, but she still called Dee and told her that I refused to let her talk to the kids. Dee was required to follow up on every one of Trisha's complaints and there were a lot of them.

Trisha would call while the kids were napping; and although I offered to wake them up, she declined. Then she would report me again for not allowing them to talk to her. She would not even ask to talk to Zander because he could not talk, but he still wanted to listen and hold the phone and would throw a fit if he did not get a turn. I would tell her Zander was listening, but she would not talk to him. I would monitor her calls and put the kids on speaker phone.

She would say to Arianna, "Don't cry, baby."

To which Arianna would respond, "I'm not crying."

Then she would say things like, "Do they hurt you? Don't let them hurt you."

Arianna said, "They don't hurt me, silly."

Then she just set the phone down and walked away to the table to eat her crackers. This infuriated Trisha. I told her Arianna no longer wanted to talk, but sure enough Trisha called Dee and told her I refused to let Arianna talk and said that I would constantly take the phone from her.

This went on for sometime when the judge finally set a once a day appointment for the children to talk to her every evening at six in the evening. I was instructed to start keeping a phone log of all of her calls. Half the time, she would hand the phone to Tina or Tina's teenage son to talk to Arianna and I would log this. We had to wait by the phone every evening for the court ordered phone call. Trisha was consistent with her appointment for about four days. Then it became twice a week, then once a week, then less than that. Nevertheless, we still had to wait by the phone every evening at six whether she called or not.

Trisha's last few phone calls I could hear desperation in her voice. For months, she had been abrasive and mean when she talked to me. She had been calling me by my first name again for some time. The last few calls she started to call me "Mama" again using her baby voice. By this time, I was wise enough to know that meant she wanted something. She confessed that "Tina" had kicked her out and she didn't have anywhere to go. She would tell me outlandish stories like she was robbed at gunpoint at the gas station and he took all her money. Another time, she told me she fell off a ladder at work and broke her ankle and couldn't work. I knew she was lying, but just let her ramble with all her details making sure to put it in my phone log. In the past, stories like this usually led into her asking for money. I could tell she didn't have the nerve to ask anymore and just hoped I would offer. I never offered again.

Trisha had now found yet another new boyfriend and was grooming his mother to be her new mama. Trisha had a trail of "mamas" behind her. I am sure each and every one had a story to tell. She needed a mama for all seasons. She needed a new mama as soon as the old one caught onto her game. It seemed a pattern that each woman she bonded with became her new "mama." I finally got it. I was just a "mama" on the trail to her next. She could write my name into her story of life and then white it out like it was never there. When she disposed of a mama, a husband or a child they no longer existed; unless, of course, they still served a purpose or were a source of attention. Eventually, Trisha just stopped calling. I have not heard from her since 2009. This is a good thing.

CHAPTER 26

Talk to Me

I had waited anxiously for this appointment. I was finally going to get some answers why Zander was not talking. I had sat over his bed and prayed for him so many times. If he would just say one sentence, one word, maybe just two words put together to express one thought to me. So far all, he could do was make sounds. He made a fair attempt to say a word to ask for things, but usually we could not understand him. We would say "show me" and he knew enough to point to a cookie or open the pantry and point to what he wanted to eat. "Say it," I would tell him. "Say the word say cereal." "Shczee Oh" was about as close as he got. I did finally figure out that he meant "cereal" and not "jello." How frustrated he must be? Here he was five years old trying to ask for something he wanted and not being able to explain it. We tried everything we could to get him to speak. We would play music and children's Bible songs in the car for him throughout the day. He would not talk but would walk to the stereo speaker and put his ear against it. He liked the sound.

We had arrived at the Psychiatrist's office. I walked from the car towards the office with Zan's usual behavior of continuously yanking on my arm in protest. It hurt my wrist. It hurt my already very sprained wrist. The doctor greeted us and went over some consent forms. She asked to take Zander alone into her exam room. Zander had seen there were toys so he didn't protest. I sat and gazed looking around the office at all of her books. I couldn't help but chuckle at all of the self-help books on the shelves. I recognized and had read several of them.

They had not been gone more than twenty minutes when the doctor returned. She sat one chair over from me. She had a relative lack of warmth about her when she said, "What I am going to tell you might make you very sad, but if you tell me it makes you so sad that you will hurt this child I will have to report you to children's services," she continued, "If you tell me it makes you so sad, you will hurt yourself I must also report you."

I sat blank faced. I was afraid to show any emotion at all. *What was she talking about reporting me?* I thought. So I sat there mirroring her cold expressionless countenance.

"Your child is mentally retarded," she continued, "he will probably never be able to care for himself independently. He will never be able to drive a car or handle his own finances. He will always need assistance to care for his needs."

How can she say that? She has only spent twenty minutes with him. *Don't cry, don't cry, don't cry*, I kept repeating in my head.

She went on, "He is not mildly retarded. He is a bit more than that. He is moderately retarded. Now there are four levels of mental retardation: mild, moderate, severe, and profound."

It was taking all of my inner strength to keep from reacting.

She went on, "He is moderately retarded, which is somewhat more than mildly retarded."

Why did she keep using the word "retarded?" I hate that word!

At that moment, Zander's future flashed before my eyes. All of the life experiences he would never have. He would never fall in love, get married, or go to college. My heart began to grieve while my face continued to remain as emotionless as hers. The doctor finished with her lengthy speech about all the things Zander would never be able to do. She asked if I had any questions and I nodded "No." No questions that I wanted *her* to answer. I wanted to get out of that office. I wanted to leave before I started to cry and she would "have to report me."

As we walked to the car, Zander was much more cooperative than he was when we had arrived. I opened the car door, buckled him in and handed him a toy. He seemed to be in great spirits. I got in the car and closed the door. Then I began to weep. I just burst out bawling, "Why God? Why does Zander have to lose his entire future because of what Trish did to him?"

I was so mad at God. I was so mad at the mother who didn't deserve to be called mother. At this exact moment from the back seat, I heard Zander begin to sing, "I've got the jowee (joy) jowee jowee jowee down in my haaawt (heart). Down in my haaawt."

He was singing! My baby was singing! He sang a whole sentence. Not just any sentence. He sang that he had joy in his heart. Here I was being all mad at God, and He decided to let Zander sing his first sentence. It was in that moment, that beautiful heaven sent moment, I knew Zander was just exactly what God wanted him to be. At that moment, God told me it was all going to be okay, that I did not need to worry. It was like God was saying, "I've got this, stop your worrying."

> Therefore I tell you, do not worry about your life, what you will eat or drink; or about your body, what you will wear. Is not life more than food, and the body more than clothes? Look at the birds of the air; they do not sow or reap or store away in barns, and yet your heavenly Father feeds them. Are you not much more valuable than they? Can any one of you by

worrying add a single hour to your life? (Matt. 6:25–34, NIV)

After this breakthrough, Zander continued to reach several new milestones. He would start putting two and three word sentences together. I would teach him to say "I want" followed by the item, object or food he wanted. His little sister was like a mini mommy. She would constantly give him praise saying "good boy" when he said a sentence. His sister was also his personal interpreter. He would say some jumbled sounds and his sister would quickly say "oh he wants juice" or a toy or whatever he wanted. She was always right too. We joked that she was fluent in Zanderin.

CHAPTER 27

Cuteness and Sweetness

Six months after the children had come to live with me, we had our final court hearing. The judge granted me permanent guardianship and the children's services case was closed. I was so relieved that the children would now have permanency and that I no longer had to fear they would be moved. Zander was doing well in pre-school and Arianna was doing well at home learning her alphabet and other things. It was hard for me when Arianna started passing Zander with her milestones. She wanted to learn. It was wonderful to see her learn things so quickly but it was also bittersweet watching her pass her brother. He was almost two years older. He should be learning these things.

For so long, I grieved over Zander's loss but finally have come to accept it. I remember having a conversation with a friend when I went down the "what if" road dreaming about what Zander would have been like "if only" I had known or they had gotten him away from his mother sooner. She stopped me in mid sentence and said, "Tammy, there is no cheese down that tunnel."

I have to remind myself of this often.

Arianna began learning the piano; and by four years old, already played several classical pieces. She was amazingly gifted. She was beginning to learn the classical piece Bach's Prelude. I jokingly told her, "If you learn the whole song, I will take you to Disneyland."

2010

Three days later, this brilliant four year old had learned all twelve pages of Bach's Prelude. After playing it for me, she said, "Okay, can we go to Disneyland tomorrow?" Arianna also loves to sing and started in a ballet class. By the time she started kindergarten, she was already reading, and if you are wondering, yes, I did take her to Disneyland.

As the children began to grow, their individual sweetness began to shine. Zander had transformed from this angry destructive little boy, to the boy who would give his only cookie to his sister because she bumped her head. Zander's teachers were starting to see bits of "adorableness" shining brighter than his aggression and destructiveness. Arianna was all heart and full of sweetness. One night, we were having pie and ice cream and as I served it I looked at her and said, "So you want the whole nine yards?"

Her response was, "Oh, no, Mommy, I just want the half nine yards, I want you to have the other half."

2013

CHAPTER 28

Today

Zander's health has been perfect, with only one exception. When he was ten years old, I decided to have his left leg surgically straightened to correct the tibial torsion that he had since birth. His left foot turned in almost forty-five degrees. It affected his walk and he really could not run. He also stumbled and fell a lot. This was a very difficult decision to make but I let him help make the decision. I explained to him it would be painful and he would have to be in a wheelchair for at least a month, but after it healed, his foot would be straight. I sat in the hospital room with him after his surgery, helping him with the intense vomiting that lasted the first two days. It broke my heart. I could not help but think of how many times Trisha had sat next to him watching him suffer in a hospital bed and relished the experience. How could a mother do that? Zander's surgery was a great success. Recently, I took him to the park and watched as he and his sister raced across the grass. Just like the joy I felt when he began to talk, I was quickened with joy watching him finally able to run.

Although Zander will always have special needs, he continues to make reach one milestone after another. He is now twelve years old. He has had several years of speech therapy and he talks! He talks about everything. He will talk about airplanes, trains, boats, the titanic, the Coast Guard, and will tell you every thing he knows on a subject. When he was in kindergarten, one of the counselors at his IEP made a comment that he may never learn to read. I refused to accept this. Today he is reading at an emerging third grade level. This, in itself, is a miracle. I try not to compare him to other children but to praise God in his progress. God has done so much healing in his life. He is still hyperactive and needs a lot of redirection but all in all he is a very happy young man. His innocence is one of the most beautiful things about him.

Arianna is doing amazing as well. She has been blessed to be part of a non-profit dance theater group called Royal Stage Christian performing arts. A group that offers classes to all children regardless of their ability to pay. They focus on helping abuse survivors. She takes ballet and theater. When she was nine years old, she was in her first play and cast in the role of Dorothy in The Wizard of Oz. She did an amazing job. As I watched her in each of her performances, I couldn't help but be thankful for what God had done to save the life of this precious girl. Things could have been so very different. Today, she is ten years old. She loves to read, sing, play piano, and act.

Although we are all focused on the future, and I dream of a time when all the scars of the past are buried, we still occasionally have reminders and I see that even the children have not forgotten. While taking a theater class, Arianna was given a small role and the characters' name was Trisha. She instantly told the teacher, "You are going to have to change that name. I will not be Trisha." She still carries deep residual hurt, but continues to heal. Just a month ago, she stood up in a church, gave her testimony about what God has done in her life and sang the song, *Till I Can Make It On My Own*, recorded by Tammy Wynette and Martina McBride, and co-written by Tammy Wynette with George Richey and Billy Sherrill. This song reflects how Arianna feels about being abandoned and harmed by her birth mother and how God has carried her through it.

Arianna, performing with Royal Stage
Christian Performing Arts: 2015

Kevin has now remarried and has another beautiful daughter. Arabella is two years old. It is a new experience, being a grandmother and not having to worry if your grandchild is fed and safe. It is a new experience *just* being her grandmother. What a contrast. I often tell Becca, my daughter-in-law, how much I appreciate her for being such a wonderful mother to my granddaughter. I tell her how thankful I am that I can have a grandchild and not have to worry about whether or not she is cared for. It took a long time for me to open my heart up again, but God has given me a wonderful daughter-in-law in Becca.

As for me, I have everything I have ever dreamed of. I am still a stressed out Mom on occasion, but I no longer snap back at men at Wal-Mart. I think about the time in my life when I struggled with infertility. I remember praying to God "If you are not going to give me another child, please take this desire out of my heart." When Zander was born and I became a grandmother, I felt the desire was gone and I was content being a grandmother. Little did I know the plans God had for me and the blessings to come.

As I sat down to write their story, our story, of tragedy, trials and eventually triumph, I have reflected on the past eight years of their healing. I have reflected on some of the cute things they have done and said over the years. They never cease to amaze me with their strength and resilience. Time after time and trial after trial, God showed up and turned our trials into triumphs. These children who were once so broken and shattered, slowly with time have become whole again. I cannot say that they do not have residual brokenness from time to time, but each time something comes up God provides exactly what is needed in that moment.

CHAPTER 29

Letting Go and Moving On

It has taken me a long time to forgive Trisha for what she put these children through. By forgive, I mean letting go of my anger towards her. This was only hurting me. She has had no contact with us since 2009. This is a good thing all for of us. Although I do pray for her from time to time. I finally had to release even that to God. Just praying for her opens that wound and allows her to occupy my mind and this makes me angry again. I have given her up to God and he can do the rest.

When I think back to when Arianna first started calling me "Mama." I reminded her I was Grandma and she responded, "But I have to call *someone* Mama." Oh how that pulled on my heart strings. Then I think of when Trisha started to call me "Mama." The two are such diametrically opposing gestures. You see, Arianna did have to call someone "Mama," a name which means everything to her. Trisha, on the other hand, had to call everyone "Mama," a name which means nothing to her.

Bibliography

Feldman, Marc. Playing Sick: Untangling the Web of Factitious Disorder, Munchausen Syndrome, Munchausen by Proxy, and Malingering. New York: Rutledge Press, 2004

About the Author

Tammy Eady Walker grew up in the small farming town of Porterville, California. She now resides in Roseville California with her family. While raising her two grandchildren, she also owns and operates her own web based quilt and fabric store, Quiltcutters.com.

Tammy's grandchildren are very active in dance and theater. She currently serves on the Board of Directors for Royal Stage Christian Performing Arts (Royalstage.org), a non-profit dance theater company benefitting abuse survivors as well as the general community.

CPSIA information can be obtained
at www.ICGtesting.com
Printed in the USA
FFOW05n2238301017